P9-BYE-954

Evidence-Based Instruction in Reading

*A Professional Development
Guide to Comprehension*

Timothy V. Rasinski

Kent State University

Nancy D. Padak

Kent State University

Boston • New York • San Francisco
Mexico City • Montreal • Toronto • London • Madrid • Munich • Paris
Hong Kong • Singapore • Tokyo • Cape Town • Sydney

Executive Editor: *Aurora Martínez Ramos*
Series Editorial Assistant: *Lynda Giles*
Marketing Manager: *Danae April*
Production Editor: *Gregory Erb*
Editorial Production Service: *Publishers' Design and Production Services, Inc.*
Composition Buyer: *Linda Cox*
Manufacturing Buyer: *Linda Morris*
Electronic Composition: *Publishers' Design and Production Services, Inc.*
Cover Designer: *Kristina Mose-Libon*

For related titles and support materials, visit our online catalog at
www.ablongman.com.

Copyright © 2008 Pearson Education, Inc.

All rights reserved. No part of the material protected by this copyright notice may
be reproduced or utilized in any form or by any means, electronic or mechanical,
including photocopying, recording, or by any information storage and retrieval
system, without written permission from the copyright owner.

To obtain permission(s) to use material from this work, please submit a written
request to Allyn and Bacon, Permissions Department, 75 Arlington Street, Boston,
MA 02116 or fax your request to 617-848-7320.

Between the time website information is gathered and then published, it is not
unusual for some sites to have closed. Also, the transcription of URLs can result in
typographical errors. The publisher would appreciate notification where these
errors occur so that they may be corrected in subsequent editions.

ISBN-10: 0-205-45627-8
ISBN-13: 978-0-205-45627-7

Library of Congress Cataloging-in-Publication Data

Rasinski, Timothy V.
    Evidence-based instruction in reading : a professional development guide to
comprehension / Timothy V. Rasinski, Nancy D. Padak.
        p.   cm.
    Includes bibliographical references.
    ISBN-13: 978-0-205-45627-7 (alk. paper)
    ISBN-10: 0-205-45627-8 (alk. paper)
    1. Reading comprehension—Study and teaching.   I. Padak, Nancy.
II. Title.

    LB1050.45.R37 2008
    372.47—dc22

                                                                    2007019717

Printed in the United States of America

10   9   8   7   6   5   4   3   RRD-VA   11   10

Photo Credits: Pages 1, 87: Image 100; p. 15: Ellen B. Senisi; pp. 55, 73:
IndexOpen.

About the Authors

Timothy V. Rasinski is a Professor of Education in the Department of Teaching, Leadership, and Curriculum Studies. He teaches graduate and undergraduate courses in literacy education. His major interests include working with children who find reading difficult, phonics and reading fluency instruction, and teacher development in literacy education. He has published over 100 articles and 10 books on various aspects of reading education. Dr. Rasinski is past editor of *The Reading Teacher* and is currently an editor for the *Journal of Literacy Research*. He has served as president of the College Reading Association and he currently serves on the Board of Directors of the International Reading Association. He earned bachelor degrees in economics and education at the University of Akron and the University of Nebraska at Omaha. His master's degree in special education also comes from the University of Nebraska at Omaha. Dr. Rasinski was awarded the Ph.D. from The Ohio State University.

Nancy D. Padak is a Distinguished Professor of Education at Kent State University where she directs the Reading and Writing Center and teaches graduate courses in literacy education and recently received the honor of Kent State University Distinguished Professor. She was a part of the team that wrote the initial grant to fund the state literacy resource center at Kent State University–Ohio Literacy Resource Center (OLRC) and has been a middle school and high school classroom teacher and administrator in a large urban school district. She frequently works with teachers and has written or edited a dozen books and more than 100 scholarly articles. Professor Padak is a past College Reading Association President and a former editor of *The Reading Teacher*. She currently edits the *Journal of Literacy Research*. She has three grown children: Katie, Mike, and Matt. Her husband Gary is Dean of Undergraduate Studies at Kent State.

Among us, we have been teachers and teacher educators for nearly 100 years! During this time, we have developed deep and abiding respect for teachers and trust in their ability to offer their students the very best possible instruction. Yet we also agree with librarian John Cotton Dana (1856–1929), who said, "Who dares to teach must never cease to learn."

Our careers have been marked by continual learning. We dedicate this book to all who have taught us and all whom we have taught— all who have dared to teach.

NP
TR
MM
EN
BZ

Contents

Series Introduction

Evidence-Based Instruction in Reading:
A Professional Development Guide

Better than a thousand days of diligent study is one day spent with a great teacher.

JAPANESE PROVERB

*L*earning to read is perhaps a young child's greatest school accomplishment. Of course, reading is the foundation for success in all other school subjects. Reading is critical to a person's own intellectual development, later economic success, and the pleasure that is to be found in life.

Similarly, teaching a child to read is one of the greatest accomplishments a teacher can ever hope for. And yet, reading and teaching reading are incredibly complex activities. The reading process involves elements of a person's psychological, physical, linguistic, cognitive, emotional, and social world. Teaching reading, of course, involves all these and more. Teachers must orchestrate the individuality of each child they encounter; the physical layout of the classroom and attendant materials; their own colleagues, parents, and school administration; the school's specified curriculum; and their own style of teaching! The popular cliché that "teaching reading is not rocket science" perhaps underestimates the enormity of the task of teaching children to read.

The complexity of teaching reading can be, quite simply, overwhelming. How does a teacher teach and find mastery of the various skills in reading, attending to the school and state curricular guidelines, using an appropriate variety of materials, while simultaneously meeting the individual needs of all children in the classroom? We think that it was because of the enormous complexity of this task that many teachers resorted to prepackaged reading programs to provide the structure and sequence for a given grade level. Basal reading programs, for example, provide some assurance that at least some of the key skills and content for reading are covered within a given period of time.

The problem with prepackaged programs is that they are not sensitive to the culture of the classroom, school, and community, the individual children in the classroom, and the instructional style of the teacher. The one-size-fits-all approach adopted by such programs—with, of course, the best of intentions—resulted in programs that met the minimal needs of the students, that lacked the creative flair that only a teacher can give a program, and that absolved teachers of a good deal of the accountability for teaching their students. If children failed to learn to read, it was the fault of the program.

The fact of the matter is that many children failed to learn to read up to expectations using prepackaged programs. The results of periodic assessments of U.S. students' reading achievement, most notably the National Assessment of Educational Progress, have demonstrated little, if any, growth in student reading achievement over the past 30 years. This lack of growth in literacy achievement is at least partially responsible for equally dismal results in student growth in other subject areas that depend highly on a student's ability to read.

The National Reading Panel Report

Having noticed this disturbing trend, the National Reading Panel (NRP) was formed by the United States Congress in 1996 and given the mandate of reviewing the scientific research related to reading and determining those areas that science has shown have the greatest promise for improving reading achievement in the elementary grades. In 2000, the NRP came out with its findings. Essentially, the panel found that the existing scientific research points to five particular areas of reading that have the greatest promise of increasing reading achievement: phonemic awareness, phonics and word decoding, reading fluency, vocabulary, and reading comprehension. Additionally, the NRP indicated that investments in teachers, through professional development activities, hold promise of improving student reading achievement.

The findings of the NRP have been the source of considerable controversy, yet they have been used by the federal and state governments, as well as local school systems, to define and mandate reading instruction. In particular, the federal Reading First program has mandated that any school receiving funds from Reading First must embed within its reading curriculum direct and systematic teaching of phonemic awareness, phonics, reading fluency, vocabulary, and comprehension. The intent of the mandate, of course, is to provide the instruction that is based on best evidence of a positive impact on students' reading achievement.

Although we may argue about certain aspects of the findings of the National Reading Panel, in particular what it left out of its report of effective instructional principles, we find ourselves in solid agreement with the panel that the five elements that it identified are indeed critical to success in learning to read.

Phonemic awareness is crucial to early reading development. Students must develop an ability to think about the sounds of language and to manipulate those sounds in various ways—to blend sounds, to segment words into sounds, and so on. An inability to deal with language sounds in this way will set the stage for difficulty in phonics and word decoding. To sound out a word, which is essentially what phonics requires of students, readers must have adequate phonemic awareness. Yet, some estimates indicate that as many as 20 percent of young children in the United States do not have sufficient phonemic awareness to profit fully from phonics instruction.

Phonics, or the ability to decode written words in text, is clearly essential for reading. Students who are unable to accurately decode at least 90 percent of the words they encounter while reading will have difficulty gaining appropriate meaning from what they read. We prefer to expand the notion of phonics to word decoding. Phonics, or using the sound–symbol relationship between letters and words, is, without doubt, an important way to solve unknown words. However, there are other methods to decode written words. These include attending to the prefixes, suffixes, and base elements of longer words; examining words for rimes (word families) and other letter patterns; using meaningful context to determine unknown words; dividing longer words into smaller parts through syllabication; and making words part of one's sight vocabulary, words recognized instantly and by sight. Good readers are able to employ all of these strategies and more. Appropriately, instruction needs to be aimed at helping students develop proficiency in learning to decode words using multiple strategies.

Reading fluency refers to the ability to read words quickly, as well as accurately, and with appropriate phrasing and expression. Fluent readers are able to decode words so effortlessly that they can direct their cognitive resources away from the low-level decoding task and to the more important meaning-making or comprehension part of reading. For a long time, fluency was a relatively neglected area of the reading curriculum. In recent years, however, educators have come to realize that although fluency deals with the ability to efficiently and effortlessly decode words, it is critical to good reading comprehension and needs to be part of any effective reading curriculum.

Word and concept meaning is the realm of *vocabulary*. Not only must readers be able to decode or sound out words but they must also know what these words mean. Instruction aimed at expanding students' repertoire of word meanings and deepening their understanding of already known words is essential to reading success. Thus, vocabulary instruction is an integral part of an effective instructional program in reading.

Accurate and fluent decoding of words, coupled with knowledge of word meanings, may seem to ensure *comprehension*. However, there is more to it than that. Good readers also actively engage in constructing meaning, beyond individual words, from what they read. That is, they engage in meaning-constructing strategies while they read. These include ensuring that readers employ their background knowledge for the topics they encounter in reading. It also means that they ask questions, make predictions, and create mental images while they read. Additionally, readers monitor their reading comprehension and know when to stop and check things out when things begin to go awry—that is, when readers become aware that they are not making adequate sense out of what they are reading. These are just some of the comprehension strategies and processes good readers use while they read to ensure that they understand written texts. These same strategies must be introduced and taught to students in an effective reading instruction program.

Phonemic awareness, phonics/decoding, reading fluency, vocabulary, and comprehension are the five essential elements of effective reading programs identified by the National Reading Panel. We strongly agree with the findings of the NRP—these elements must be taught to students in their reading program.

Rather than get into in-depth detail on research and theory related to these topics, our intent in this series is to provide you with a collection of simple, practical, and relatively easy-to-implement instructional strategies, proven through research and actual practice, for teaching each of the five essential components. We think you will find the books in this series readable and practical. Our hope is that you will use these books as a set of handbooks for developing more effective and engaging reading instruction for all your students.

Professional Development in Literacy

Effective literacy instruction requires teachers to be knowledgeable, informed professionals capable of assessing student needs and responding to those needs with an assortment of instructional strategies. Whether you are new to the field or a classroom veteran, ongoing professional development is imperative. Professional development influences instructional practices which, in turn, affect student achievement (Wenglinsky, 2000). Effective professional development is not simply an isolated program or activity; rather, it is an ongoing, consistent learning effort where links between theoretical knowledge and the application of that knowledge to daily classroom practices are forged in consistent and meaningful ways (Renyi, 1998).

Researchers have noted several characteristics of effective professional development: It must be grounded in research-based practices; it must be collaborative, allowing teachers ample opportunities to share knowledge, as well as teaching and learning challenges, among colleagues; and it must actively engage teachers in assessing, observing, and responding to the learning and development of their students (Darling-Hammond & McLaughlin, 1995). This professional development series, *Evidence-Based Instruction in Reading: A Professional Development Guide* is intended to provide a roadmap for systematic, participatory professional development initiatives.

Using the Books

The *Evidence-Based Instruction in Reading* series consists of five professional development books, each addressing one major component of literacy instruction identified by the National Reading Panel and widely accepted in the field as necessary for effective literacy programs: phonemic awareness, phonics, vocabulary, fluency, and comprehension. These five components are not, by any means, the only components needed for effective literacy instruction. Access to appropriate reading materials, productive home–school connections, and a desire to learn to read and write are also critical pieces of the literacy puzzle. It is our hope, however, that by focusing in depth on each of the five major literacy components, we can provide educators and professional development facilitators with concrete guidelines and suggestions for enhancing literacy instruction. Our hope is that teachers who read, reflect, and act on the information in these books will be more able to provide effective instruction in each of the five essential areas of reading.

Each book is intended to be used by professional development facilitators, be they administrators, literacy coaches, reading specialists, and/or classroom teachers, and program participants as they engage in professional development initiatives or in-service programs within schools or school districts. The use of the series can be adapted to meet the specific needs and goals of a group of educators. For example, a school may choose to hold a series of professional development sessions on each of the five major components of literacy instruction; it may choose to focus in depth on one or two components that are most relevant to its literacy program; or it may choose to focus on specific aspects, such as assessment or instructional strategies, of one or more of the five areas.

The books may also be useful in professional book club settings. An icon, included at spots for book club discussion, marks times when you might wish to share decisions about your own classroom to get colleagues' feedback. You might also want to discuss issues or solve problems with colleagues. Appendix A lists several other possible book club activities. These are listed by chapter and offer opportunities to delve into issues mentioned in the chapters in greater depth. It is important that, in collaboration with teachers, professional development needs be carefully assessed so that the appropriate content can be selected to meet those needs.

Overview of Book Content

To begin each book in the series, Chapter 1 presents a literature review that defines the literacy component to be addressed in that book, explains why this component is important in the context of a complete and balanced literacy program, and synthesizes key research findings that underlie the recommendations for evidence-based instructional practices that follow in subsequent chapters. The conclusion of Chapter 1 invites professional development program participants to analyze, clarify, extend, and discuss the material presented in this chapter.

Chapter 2 outlines general principles for instruction. Participants are asked to evaluate their own instructional practices and to plan for refinement of those practices based on their students' needs. Each suggested instructional strategy in this chapter is based on the research presented in Chapter 1 and includes the purpose, necessary materials, and procedures for implementation. Ideas for engaging professional development participants in extended discussions related to phonemic awareness, phonics, vocabulary, fluency, or comprehension are offered at the end of Chapter 2.

Chapter 3 begins by presenting broad themes for effective assessment such as focusing on critical information; looking for patterns of behavior; recognizing developmental progressions; deciding how much assessment information is needed; using instructional situations for assessment purposes; using assessment information to guide instruction; and sharing assessment information with children and families. At the end of Chapter 3, professional development participants are asked to evaluate their current assessment practices, draw conclusions about needed change, and develop plans for change. The conclusion of the chapter provides vignettes and questions designed to generate collaborative discussion about and concrete ways to enhance connections between assessment and classroom instruction.

Chapter 4 invites participants to think beyond classroom-based strategies by examining activities that can be recommended to families to support children's development of phonemic awareness, phonics, vocabulary, fluency, and comprehension at home. The final chapter provides a variety of print- and web-based resources to support instruction in phonemic awareness, phonics, vocabulary, fluency, or comprehension.

Together, the information and activities included in these books, whether used as is or selectively, will foster careful consideration of research-based practice. Professional development participants will learn about the research that supports their current practices and will be guided to identify areas for improvement in their classroom programs.

The need for new programs and methods for teaching reading is questionable. What is without question is the need for great teachers of reading—teachers who are effective, inspiring, and knowledgeable about children and reading. This series of books is our attempt to guide teachers into a deeper understanding of their craft and art—to help already good teachers become the great teachers that we need.

Introduction

Comprehension

Comprehension is widely recognized as the goal of reading. But what does it mean to comprehend in reading? Do readers comprehend when they have understood what they read? What does the term *understand* mean? Do readers comprehend when they can retell the information they have read in a passage? Do readers comprehend when they can relate the content they have read to their own lives? Do readers comprehend when they can apply the information to some other task? Do readers comprehend when they can provide information that is not directly or specifically stated in the text? Or do readers comprehend when they can appreciate the beauty of the language they encounter while reading?

To some extent, all these criteria are accurate descriptions of comprehension. There are, we are sure, many other conceptions of comprehension. Comprehension is a concept that is tricky to define, yet it is also something that we recognize when we have achieved it. We know when we have understood what we have read, but it is often difficult to explain what it means to comprehend.

Similarly, we know what it means to comprehend when we read, but do we really know how we develop this skill and how we might impart this important skill to others, our students? Seminal research by Dolores Durkin (1978) found that teachers struggled with the idea of actually teaching comprehension to students. We have a good sense of what comprehension is, we know that it is important for reading and other intellectual tasks, yet we often are challenged by the daunting task of teaching it to our students.

Clearly, the components of reading described in the previous books in the series are important for comprehension. Readers need to be able to decode words accurately (phonics), read automatically or effortlessly with appropriate prosody or expression (fluency), and know what the words mean (vocabulary). And phonemic awareness is an important precondition for the ability to decode words. But we all know that there are readers who can read words accurately, automatically, expressively, and know the meaning of all the words in the passage, and yet fail to have adequate comprehension of the passage itself. Something else needs to happen for comprehension to occur; we refer to this something else as *comprehension dispositions and strategies.*

In order to get a sense of your own ideas about comprehension, try your hand at the following questions about comprehension:

1. _____ Comprehension is best taught
   a. through basal reading programs
   b. mainly through stories and narrative texts
   c. through lively teacher-led discussions of stories that students read
   d. through read-aloud
   e. none of the above

2. _____ Schema theory refers to
   a. text structure
   b. readers' background knowledge
   c. vocabulary knowledge
   d. literal comprehension

3. _____ Inferential comprehension refers to
   a. understanding the main idea and details of a passage
   b. the ability to develop a succinct summary of a text
   c. appreciating the aesthetic qualities of texts
   d. the ability to make reasonable guesses about material that is not explicitly stated in the text

4. _____ Expository texts are
   a. informational in nature
   b. essentially narratives
   c. poems and other forms of rhythmical texts
   d. all the above

5. _____ Metacognition refers to the reader's
   a. understanding of meaning implied in a passage
   b. background knowledge for a passage
   c. comprehension of poetic texts
   d. awareness of his or her own reading process
   e. all of the above

6. _____ Which is *not* generally considered a form of exposition?
   a. narration
   b. enumeration
   c. chronology
   d. cause and effect

7. _____ Students demonstrate comprehension when they
   a. can retell the main ideas or events of a passage
   b. make inferences about the motives of the main character
   c. can make critical judgments about the passage and its various features
   d. can remake the passage into another form such as a script or poem
   e. all the above

8. _____ True or False: Understanding and using charts, graphs, diagrams, maps, and other forms of graphically presented information is part of the domain of reading comprehension.

(The answer key is at the end of this section.)

How did you do on our brief pretest? Whether you did well or struggled with some of the items, we hope that this quiz helps you see that comprehension is a pretty complex issue that involves several mental processes; applies to many text types (genre) and features; is individual but also has a strong social dimension; involves what happens before, during, and after reading; and, most importantly, can be taught and nurtured by teachers.

As you prepare for your journey into reading comprehension through this professional development program, we invite you to consider and discuss with colleagues the following items that may help frame your own comprehension and response to the material in this book. Take time to jot notes about these aspects of the literacy program you have now and the literacy program you would like to have for all your students, especially in regard to reading comprehension.

- Describe the methods and materials you now use for teaching reading comprehension to your students.

   _____

   _____

   _____

   _____

- What basic principles guide your reading comprehension instruction?

  _____

  _____

  _____

  _____

- How do you identify (assess) students who have difficulty comprehending what they read?

  _____

  _____

  _____

  _____

- How do you determine the source of their comprehension difficulty? How do you know it is due to, say, a lack of reading fluency or a difficulty in applying reading comprehension strategies?

  _____

  _____

  _____

  _____

- How do you provide differential comprehension instruction for students of differential needs?

  _____

  _____

  _____

  _____

- How do you involve parents in developing students' reading comprehension?

  _____

  _____

  _____

  _____

- Who is the reading teacher (from the past or present) that you admire the most? What did this reading teacher do that so impressed you?

  _____

  _____

  _____

  _____

- What would be your first step to becoming a better teacher of reading comprehension?

  _____

  _____

  _____

  _____

The chapters that follow will engage you in considering the concepts and ideas framed in the preceding questions. This book is not intended to be a comprehensive treatment of reading comprehension, nor is it intended to provide you with all you need to teach reading comprehension to your students. Rather, we will present you with up-to-date information about reading comprehension, based on scientific evidence, but presented from a teacher's point of view. Moreover, our hope is that through our presentation you will think more deeply, collaboratively, critically, and creatively about helping your students become better comprehenders of the material they read.

Chapter 1 presents an overview of the current research and professional literature on reading comprehension. Research-based and scholarly answers are provided for important questions such as what comprehension is and what the various dimensions or components of comprehension and comprehension instruction are. The chapter ends with an invitation to analyze, clarify, extend, discuss, and apply information presented in the chapter.

In Chapter 2, the heart of the book, we focus on research-based instructional practices for teaching reading comprehension. We take our cue from the National Reading Panel (NRP) (2000) that identified a set of specific instructional practices for teaching reading comprehension. However, we go beyond the NRP and describe other instructional practices that have been validated by empirical research and researchers as effective instructional practices for reading comprehension.

Chapter 3 deals with assessment of comprehension. Assessment and progress monitoring are clearly important parts of reading instruction. However, assessment takes time and time given to assessment is time taken away from instruction. Thus, we examine ways to look at assessment that are simple and time efficient for teachers and students.

We move beyond the classroom in Chapter 4 and consider ways in which we can continue reading comprehension development at home and at times when school is not in session. Although parents and other family members may not be trained in the technical aspects of reading and comprehension instruction, there are many things they can do to help their children improve their ability to make sense of text.

Chapter 5 provides you with resources for teaching reading comprehension, including professional resources on comprehension, trade books for children that lend themselves to various aspects of comprehension, and web resources that may assist you in becoming a better teacher.

Throughout the book you will find ample room to make notes about various aspects of planning and implementing effective comprehension instruction. We encourage you to use these spaces to record reactions, insights, and ideas that are particularly relevant to your own instruction and situation. You will find these notes invaluable as you begin to develop your own concrete plan to make comprehension instruction more effective for all your students.

Answer Key: 1–e; 2–b; 3–d, 4–a, 5–d; 6–a; 7–e; 8–T

CHAPTER 1

Reading Comprehension: Definitions, Research, and Considerations

2

CHAPTER 1

*Reading
Comprehension:
Definitions,
Research, and
Considerations*

*I*n defining any literacy-related term, perhaps the first place to look is the *Literacy Dictionary* (Harris & Hodges, 1995). The entry for *comprehension* is one of the longest in the book. Multiple definitions are offered. One deals with the reconstructing of the message of a text. Another focuses on the understanding of individual words; still another deals with the symbolic meaning of an experience. We feel that the following definition offers the most comprehensive and instructionally useful definition of *reading comprehension:*

> [Reading comprehension is] the construction of the meaning of a written or spoken communication through a reciprocal, holistic interchange of ideas between the interpreter and the message. . . . The presumption here is that meaning resides in the intentional problem-solving, thinking processes of the interpreter, . . . that the content of the meaning is influenced by that person's prior knowledge and experience. (Harris & Hodges, 1995, p. 39)

Noteworthy in this definition is the word *construction*. Reading comprehension is not simply the recall or regurgitation of information encountered in text. *Reciprocal* implies that that the reader brings something to reading comprehension–it's not just the information in the text; the information that the reader already possesses also influences the construction of meaning. And *problem-solving, thinking processes* suggest that the reader is actively involved in attempting to construct meaning. This also insinuates that the interpretation or understanding that a reader may construct may not be the same understanding constructed by another reader of the same text. Readers filter the text through their own background knowledge, biases, and other predispositions that affect how they interpret text.

Indeed, this is the reason that every four years, voters across the United States can hear the very same speeches, read the same editorials, and examine the same analyses by experts and yet be nearly equally divided in their vote for president. They filter all that information through their own existing knowledge, experiences, biases, and other predispositions to come to quite different interpretations on who should be the next leader of the country.

Background Knowledge

CHAPTER 1

*Reading
Comprehension:
Definitions,
Research, and
Considerations*

The definition presented suggests that a key component of comprehension is the background or prior knowledge that a reader brings to the reading task. That background knowledge can include knowledge of the format and conventions of reading and the printed page, it can include an understanding of the purpose for the reading, and, perhaps most especially, it needs to include some knowledge of the content of the material to be read. Have you ever tried reading a passage for which you either have little background knowledge or are not aware that you should be using it? Understanding that passage can be quite a daunting task.

The importance of background knowledge in reading has been demonstrated in a program of study and research termed *schema theory* (Anderson & Pearson, 1984; Rumelhart, 1980). According to schema theory, comprehension is not only a bottom-up process driven by sensory input of letters, words, and text; it is also a top-down process in which the reader brings his or her own knowledge on a topic and problem-solving skills to the task of making meaning from text. Many studies have demonstrated that readers' background knowledge profoundly affects how well they comprehend what they read (e.g., Adams & Bertram, 1980; Durkin, 1981; Pearson et al., 1979). Moreover, background knowledge is particularly important for inferential comprehension, which involves constructing understandings of information that is not directly stated in the passage but implied. This is because the reader is able to relate the implied information to his or her own background knowledge and prior experiences. Take, for example, the following sentence:

Carefully the shadowy character walked down the deserted alley.

For this sentence create a mental image and answer the following questions: What time of day is it? Is the person who is walking down the alley male or female? What is the age of the person walking? Why is he or she walking down the alley? What is this person feeling? What does the alley look like? What do you see when you look to the left and right? Red brick walls? Do you see a metal fire escape hanging from one of the walls? Is the alley made up of broken concrete? Are there puddles of water on the ground? Are there any smells? Are there any noises you hear?

4
....

CHAPTER 1

*Reading
Comprehension:
Definitions,
Research, and
Considerations*

You probably did not find it difficult to respond to these questions. Where did you get the information to make your responses? Most likely you pulled that information from your background knowledge. You probably have a schema in your mind for walking down a deserted alley—maybe it comes from actually experiencing such an event or perhaps it comes from watching movies in which a scene such as that is portrayed. No matter how you developed your schema, you used it to infer (or make an educated guess about) information that was directly stated in the sentence. The meaning you have created, even if some of the meaning turns out later to be incorrect, is much more elaborate than the meaning of a reader who only passively read the sentence and went no further than understanding the words themselves.

Clearly, comprehension is more than a matter of reading the words. It needs to involve the reader in actively making decisions, solving problems, and using background knowledge in an attempt to make sense of the passage.

Comprehension Strategies

The reader and what the reader brings to the reading task are important for comprehension. But let's face it—the reader has to be reading something for reading comprehension to occur. The text and the information in the text are also important. Readers need to process the information in the text. This is done, to some extent, through the fluent decoding and understanding of words in the text. These are the bottom-up processes that are driven primarily by one's visual and auditory senses.

In our view, both processes are important, and an interaction between the bottom-up and top-down processes provides the optimal conditions for comprehension to actually take place. A common description of reading comprehension states that comprehension is the process of making connections between the new information in the text and the known information in the reader's head. This description implies that there are strategies that readers use to make the connections (or interact) between the text and their own background knowledge or schemata. These interactions lead to the new schemata (adding to one's background knowledge) or to greater elaborations of existing schemata (making modifications to what one already knows). When schemata are built or altered as a result of these interactive comprehension processes, new learning or comprehension takes place.

These interactive processes that make connections between what the reader knows and the information presented in a text are what we call *comprehension processes*. Your own process of comprehending while you read is so well developed and automatic that you may not be fully aware of the fact that you are actively using your own comprehension strategies while reading. But the fact of the matter is that if you are a good comprehender, you are using strategies to help make sense of what you read.

If you created a mental image while you read the sentence about walking down the alley, you put a comprehension strategy to work. Have you ever read something and said to yourself, "I've had an experience like that in my own life," or "This reminds me of something that I read about a few days ago." Those are both comprehension strategies. Do you ever find yourself thinking about what may happen in the next chapter or part of text? That is a comprehension strategy. Have you ever found yourself retelling or summarizing a passage to a spouse or friend or colleague? When reading an information book, has the passage ever led to you to ask questions that you would like to answer? Or have you ever jotted questions or comments in the margin of a book while reading? Those are all comprehension strategies. And, have you ever come to the point in reading where you discover that you are not understanding the passage as well as you think you should and you decide to reread the passage or to look up some words in the passage for which you are not quite sure of the meaning? That, too, is a comprehension strategy. Indeed, there are many strategies that readers use to help create meaning to texts. Some strategies are used more often than others—some are used with particular kinds of texts, and some are used with all texts. But the fact of the matter is that reading is an active process of constructing meaning that goes well beyond simply reading the words and knowing what the words mean. It is an elaborate dance between the reader and the text in which the reader attempts to filter (or mold) the information from the text through (using) his or her own background knowledge so that the new information can fit within the existing knowledge structures or schema that the reader has in place.

In recent years literacy scholars have attempted to identify comprehension strategies that have been shown through research to facilitate comprehension. In particular, the National Reading Panel (2000) has identified a set of set of research-validated strategies.

6

CHAPTER 1

*Reading
Comprehension:
Definitions,
Research, and
Considerations*

These include mental imagery, comprehension monitoring, cooperative learning, graphic organizers and story structure, question generation and answering, and summarization. Other scientific reviews of the comprehension and learning research have identified other promising strategies for promoting textual understanding. In particular, Marzano, Pickering, and Pollock (2001) noted that identifying similarities and differences, constructing nonlinguistic representations, and generating and testing hypotheses have strong potential for improving students' learning through text. In their research into effective reading instruction, Pressley and Wharton-McDonald (2002) noted several additional strategies they call transactional in nature that have been shown to improve comprehension. In addition to the ones previously mentioned, they identified responding to texts based on prior knowledge and interpreting text. In Chapter 2 we provide a more detailed explanation of each of these processes and suggestions for making these strategies come to life in the classroom.

Levels of Comprehension

Comprehension is indeed a complex process, and there are many ways to examine comprehension. One helpful way to look at comprehension is through the levels or types of comprehension readers do when reading. Thomas Barrett (Clymer, 1968) developed a simple three-level taxonomy that is useful in understanding how readers comprehend. The first level is *literal or factual comprehension*. This refers to the simple understanding of the information that is explicitly stated in the text. In the sentence, *The dog chased the three children across the field,* the literal comprehension involves knowing that it was a dog that was chasing, that the dog was chasing three children, and that the chase occurred in a field. Applying the definition of comprehension presented earlier in this chapter, literal comprehension is heavily reliant on the information presented in the text.

Barrett's second level, *inferential comprehension*, refers to information that relies on information that is implied, or not explicitly stated in the text. In the sentence example, inferential comprehension allows the reader to infer or guess what kind of dog was chasing the children, if the dog was barking or not, the ages and gender of the children, and the nature of the field that the children and dog were crossing. These pieces of information were not explicitly stated in the text; however, the reader could call up his or her background knowledge about dogs chasing children to make reasonable guesses about the scene. These are inferences that most readers can agree on. Most readers, for example, would agree that the dog was barking and that the children were running. From the definition of comprehension presented earlier, inferential comprehension can be seen as relying significantly on both the text and the reader.

Barrett's third level, *critical or evaluative comprehension*, involves the reader making judgments about various aspects of the text—the literary quality of the text, the competency of the author, the righteousness of the characters and their actions, and so on. This level of comprehension obviously relies on the text, but to an even greater extent, it requires the reader to make personal judgments about the text. In a sense, these are inferences also, but they are highly dependent on the individual and unique background of the reader. One reader may love the passage, and another may have disliked it intensely. Who is correct in their judgment? We'd have to say both readers. A fine example of critical comprehension is the presidential election that we referred to earlier. Although the positions, backgrounds, and expert opinions may be known by the entire electorate, the decision or judgment made by the voters is usually widely split— never unanimous.

All three levels of comprehension are important and need to be fostered. In the past, however, literal comprehension was the primary focus of instruction. Perhaps that is because literal comprehension is easier for a teacher to deal with—the facts are indisputable, and questions that focus on literal comprehension are simple to develop and evaluate. Literal comprehension, however, requires little in the way of engaged thinking and problem solving on the part of the reader.

It is the second and third levels of comprehension, inferential and critical, that challenge the reader to actively engage his or her background knowledge and reasoning skills to construct meaning— meaning that is not simply stated in the written text but meaning that can be discussed and debated. These are the levels that make reading comprehension a thinking task rather than simply a recall task. Research into effective classroom instruction in reading has found that effective teachers are more likely to focus on inferential and critical comprehension, the higher levels of comprehension, than less effective teachers.

The nature of the text students are asked to read also needs to be given consideration for comprehension instruction. First, teachers should ensure that the text is readable for students—it must be written at a level that is commensurate with students' reading skills. Teachers also need to make sure that the general content of the passage is appropriate for students, and that the general format (font, print size, headings, graphics, etc.) is within students' ability to handle.

Perhaps most important, teachers need to be sensitive to the general type or genre of text given to students to read. Elementary classrooms tend to have stories or narrative as the predominant genre. This is usually followed by informational or expository text. Bringing up the rear are other forms of text such as poetry, rhetoric, scripts, song lyrics, jokes and riddles, and so on. Each of these genres poses different comprehension demands on the reader. For example, the structure of texts varies by genre—narratives tend to be linear and chronological in their structure; informational texts tend to be hierarchical and logical in their structure. Poetry can have a different structure than the previous two. Students expecting to read narrative but who are given informational material may have considerable difficulty in making meaning.

Optimal reading instruction provides students with exposure to a wide variety of text types and genre. The job of the teacher, then, is to help students work through the variety of text types and structures they may encounter, from the large and obvious differences between texts to the more subtle and nuanced variations that may still have a profound impact on if and how a reader comprehends a text.

Teaching Comprehension

As you can probably infer from the previous presentation, the teaching of comprehension can be quite involved and complex. Teachers need to ensure that students have basic prerequisite decoding and fluency skills and sufficient vocabulary and background knowledge for the text to be read; they need to choose texts appropriately—the right level of difficulty and a good balance between narrative, informational, and other genres; and they need to choose and be knowledgeable about various comprehension strategies. Beyond these, however, teachers need to be aware of the appropriate level of support or scaffolding students need in the process of reading and learning to use various comprehension strategies.

Pearson and Gallagher (1983) propose a model of instructional support, called the Gradual Release of Responsibility Model, that we find very compelling and that we hope you will seriously consider in your own approach to instruction. The model proposes three levels or phases of teacher–student responsibility in any sort of learning, but in particular learning to comprehend from text. In the initial phase, the teacher takes on the bulk of the responsibility for the lesson as she or he models for students the processes and strategies that students are to learn. In practice, this is done by the teacher describing the process or strategy, presenting analogies of the process from other tasks with which students are familiar, and implementing and displaying the process for students to view on their own. Throughout this modeling, the teacher often comments on his or her own implementation—in other words, what the teacher is doing and what he or she is thinking. In this process, often called *think aloud*, the teacher takes that which is normally invisible and makes it visible through actions and verbalizations. The teacher may have to model the process in this way several times over the course of several days.

The second phase of the model is joint responsibility, where both the teacher and students take responsibility for task implementation. They may do the task together or do different portions of the task. Or students may engage in the task under the watchful eye of the teacher who observes, gives feedback and evaluation, and encourages student work. Again, the guided practice may require a number of attempts over several days. Throughout the second phase of the model, the teacher is slowly pulling away from the task, allowing the students to take more and more responsibility.

The third and final phase has the students in complete control of the implementation of the process. They work independently with minimal support from the teacher, unless requested. The goal for the students is to develop skill and fluency in the implementation of a particular strategy and integrate it into their own repertoire of reading strategies. At this point, the students have developed ownership of that strategy and should be able to apply whenever they feel necessary.

Comprehension is not something that happens automatically in the mind of the reader as he or she engages with print, even

10
....
CHAPTER 1

*Reading
Comprehension:
Definitions,
Research, and
Considerations*

though it may seem that way to adult proficient readers. Reading comprehension is an active, thoughtful, strategic, and multidimensional process that readers employ to take in new meaning from the written text and fit (or file) it into their existing knowledge structures (files). It is a process by which human beings learn. It is the job of teachers to help students become aware of, or acquire, and employ this process in their own reading.

Professional Development Suggestions

Book Club

ACED: Analysis, Clarification, Extension, Discussion

I. REFLECTION (10 to 15 minutes)

ANALYSIS:

- What, for you, were the most interesting and/or important ideas in this introduction to reading comprehension?

  _____

  _____

  _____

  _____

- What information was new to you (or different from your own prior knowledge about reading comprehension)?

  _____

  _____

  _____

  _____

CLARIFICATION:

- Did anything surprise you? Confuse you? Cause you to stop and reflect?

  _____

  _____

  _____

  _____

- Was there anything missing from or overlooked in this presentation on reading comprehension?

  _____

  _____

  _____

  _____

12

CHAPTER 1
*Reading
Comprehension:
Definitions,
Research, and
Considerations*

EXTENSION:

- What new questions or wonderings do you have about reading comprehension?

  _____

  _____

  _____

  _____

- Can you relate any information presented in this chapter to your own previous teaching experiences or to students you have taught in the past?

  _____

  _____

  _____

  _____

- What new insights do you have about reading comprehension that you developed as a result of reading this chapter?

  _____

  _____

  _____

  _____

II. DISCUSSION (20 minutes)

- Form groups of 4 to 6 members.

- Appoint a *facilitator (timer)* and *recorder*.

- Share responses. Make sure that each person has shared his or her responses to each category (Analysis/Clarification/Extension).

- Help each other with any areas of confusion.

- Answer and/or discuss questions raised by group members.

- On chart paper, the recorder should summarize the main discussion points and identify issues or questions the group would like to raise for general discussion.

13

CHAPTER 1

*Reading
Comprehension:
Definitions,
Research, and
Considerations*

III. APPLICATION (10 minutes)

- Based on your reflection and discussion, how might you apply what you have learned from this introduction to reading comprehension?

_____

_____

_____

_____

Instructional Strategies for Teaching Reading Comprehension

16
....

CHAPTER 2

Instructional
Strategies for
Teaching Reading
Comprehension

*A*s a young fifth-grade teacher, the focus of my (Tim's) reading instruction was reading comprehension. Most of my students were decent at word decoding and appeared to be average to above average in intelligence. Clearly, I had to guide my students in making sense of what they read. Yet, I was baffled about how this might be done. Comprehension was not a visible process—it occurred inside the head of the reader. Although I knew when I understood what I read, it was not clear to me what I actually did to make sense of the words I read.

And so, when I taught reading to my intermediate-grade students, I reverted to the way reading was taught to me as a fifth-grade student. We read a story, sometimes silently, often orally in round-robin fashion, and after the reading the teacher led us in a discussion of what we had read. Often that discussion entailed the teacher asking questions, usually factual questions that often required a one- or two-word response, and then calling on individual students to answer those questions. This was followed with the assignment of reading the next story in the reading program.

Although the focus of the discussion (or recitation) that I had with my students was on the meaning of the text, it became clear to me pretty quickly that I was not doing much to help my students think deeply about what they had read. In fact, all I was asking them to do was recall the basic facts of what they had read, and I was doing little more than assessing their ability to recall those literal facts. Moreover, it appeared to me that my students were minimally engaged in these discussions. They seemed barely interested in regurgitating the facts of the story that were prompted by the questions I pulled from the teacher's edition of the reading program. I knew I was not doing much to foster the kind of comprehension that led to interesting and engaging discussion and creative activities based on the essential, but often implied, meaning of the passage.

I was at a loss for how to lead students into those deeper levels of comprehension that I entered when actively engaged in reading a passage. Moreover, the teacher's manual was of little help in going deeper into meaning. I knew what I was doing was not best practice, but I did not know what I should be doing.

Apparently many teachers of the day also had similar experiences, because in the late 1970s through the 1990s reading comprehension researchers and scholars have explored how to lead students into those deeper levels of understanding. Their work has led to the groundbreaking rediscoveries of schema theory and cognitive strategies for making meaning from text. In the next section of this chapter we present a set of instructional strategies that have been verified through empirical research as holding strong promise for improving students' ability to comprehend what they read.

At the end of each section that describes a strategy we encourage you to stop, reflect on the strategy, think about how you already put the strategy into action in your classroom, and then think about new ways you may be able to foster this strategy with your students. You may wish to record your reflections and responses in writing so that you have a written record that you can go back to later. Finally, share your thoughts with a partner or in a small group, and follow that up with a more precise sharing with a larger group. The talk and responses generated from your sharing and the sharing of your colleagues can lead to even deep levels of understanding and implementation.

Before we move on to the strategies, we offer a couple caveats and suggestions. Many of the strategies and ideas we present may be a bit challenging for some students, especially those who are beginning readers. We recognize that every teacher works with students who represent a range of abilities and levels of achievement. With that in mind, then, as you go through the strategies that follow, remember that some of the strategies may simply be inappropriate for some or all of the children with whom you are working. We recognize and understand fully that the decisions on what strategies to use or not use have to be your own. Who better knows her or his students than you, the classroom teacher?

Also, please note that we present most of the comprehension strategies with the assumption that students will be reading the assigned texts on their own. Although many younger students may not be reading (or writing) independently, this should not prevent you from using many, if not most, of the strategies with them. The same comprehension strategies that are used with students while reading and writing on their own can also be employed with students who are listening to texts being read to them by their teacher or other reader and are dictating their responses. You write their replies on chart paper so that the entire instructional group can see the written response being formed through your conversion of their talk into written language. In this way, comprehension instruction is a community experience in which students, with the aid of their teacher, create meaning and respond meaningfully to texts they might not read on their own yet.

Read-aloud and dictation time, then, can (and should) easily be adapted so that you can provide students with effective comprehension instruction on relatively sophisticated texts. Even though the students may not be doing the reading or writing—they *are* doing the comprehending.

Book Club

In the previous chapter we defined reading comprehension as the process of actively making connections between new information in the text and information that is already known about the topic of the text. Thus, to comprehend means that a reader must already know something about what he or she is reading. Background or prior knowledge about the text read is essential to successful comprehension.

As a starting place, then, teachers need to ensure that their students know something about what they are reading. Even when students already have sufficient background knowledge, it is the teacher's responsibility to rekindle or remind students of that knowledge. This can occur simply with a brief presentation or discussion about the topic to be read—much like the trailer to a movie that is often presented in the upcoming features segment of a trip to the theater.

But what does a teacher do when students are not sufficiently familiar with a topic that is to be encountered in reading? The simple answer is that the teacher needs to provide students with that knowledge. This can take a variety of forms:

• You (the teacher) may simply tell students about the topic to be read. A simple illustrative presentation, coupled with strong analogies, can often lay the groundwork for successful comprehension. For example, if students will be reading about the state legislature in their social studies text, you might wish to explain that a legislature is a rule- or law-making body for the state, similar to the student council that often makes or suggests rules to be followed by the student body in school.

• In some cases, students may have some knowledge about a topic, but individually none has sufficient knowledge to handle the text. In this circumstance, you might use a simple brainstorming session in which students are asked to list what they know about a particular topic. Your role as the teacher is to elaborate on their contributions and to identify and clarify any bits of knowledge shared that may not be totally accurate.

You might want to take the brainstorming experience a bit further and work with students to organize or sort the various bits of shared information into discrete categories. For example, if students will be reading about lions, tigers, and other cats in that live in the wild, you might have the class volunteer their own knowledge on the topic. (As a member of the classroom community, be sure to add your own bits of knowledge to the growing list of information.)

Then, work with the students to sort the facts into categories, such as information on where cats in the wild live, what they eat, the nature of their family/social unit, how the young are raised, why they are hunted by humans, and so on. Later on, students can be asked to summarize their prior knowledge, using the formed categories as a general outline or organizing device.

• If students do not have prior knowledge on a topic, direct experience is the best way to provide that knowledge. So, if your students will be reading about their community, then a walk or field trip to various locations in their community will not only provide background knowledge but it will also elicit some excitement and motivation for the reading.

Although it would be nice to take a field trip with your students to France in anticipation of reading a book or chapter about France, the chances of that happening are slim to none. The next best thing to direct experience, however, is vicarious or indirect experience—to experience something through the eyes, words, documents, pictures, and sounds of others. Here is where other media—such as local museums, resource people, photographs, movies, and audiotapes—can play an important role.

When reading about World War II, for example, students can obtain oral histories of the grandparents and great-grandparents who lived through the Second World War. When reading about slavery, they can read the oral histories (slave narratives) collected by historians during the Great Depression. And when reading about the Civil War, students can find and read the personal letters sent home by soldiers who fought on both sides of the war. The Internet is a wonderful source for such material, and the new search engines available on the Internet make finding such material relatively easy.

• Even beyond movies and recorded words are written words. Reading itself, or reading done by the teacher to students (i.e., read-alouds), is perhaps the most powerful way to build students' background knowledge about particular topics. As Emily Dickinson once wrote, "There is no frigate like a book to take us lands away."

Well-chosen books, when read aloud, can build students' background knowledge, develop an interest in reading and the topic read, help develop in students a love of literary language, and build their vocabulary. The words found in literary texts that students read to students are often the well-chosen words that Isabel Beck (Beck, McKeown, & Kucan, 2002) says are the best words to build vocabulary—words students are likely to see in print but often unlikely to use in their own speech. The teacher and students can choose interesting words from a read-aloud session, put the chosen words on a class "Word Wall," and intentionally use the words in their speech and writing over the next several days. Moreover, because you are doing the reading, students can deal with more sophisticated texts that they may not be able to read on their own, thereby challenging them to comprehend or make meaning from more complex and challenging texts.

Recently in one of my undergraduate classes, during a discussion of famous figures from the twentieth century, I was shocked to find that many of my college students were not familiar with Charles Lindbergh. I remedied this situation the following day by bringing into the class the thin picture book by Robert Burleigh entitled *Flight* that told the story of Lindbergh's solo crossing of the Atlantic Ocean in an airplane in the 1920s. A picture book was able to build the background (and interest) of bright college students who had not previously stored the knowledge of Charles Lindbergh into their heads.

• A particularly powerful way to build students' background knowledge is through artifacts that may be related to a particular topic or theme that will be explored through reading. Some people call these *mini-museums, jackdaws* (a bird with a predilection for collecting items such as string and buttons and adding them to its nest), or *artifact collections*. Whatever you call them, they are a great way to start interest and build background knowledge for topics encountered in reading.

When I (Tim) taught in the intermediate grades, we spent a good deal of time talking about the Great Depression—a significant time in American history as well as a topic for which there was a rich source of children's literature. With my sixth-graders we read Irene Hunt's classic tale of the Great Depression, *No Promises in the Wind.* The first year we read the book, it became clear to me that my students were not clear what the Great Depression was all about. Some students thought it was a medical condition in which people felt profoundly sad.

To rectify this lack of background knowledge in my students, I turned to my in-laws, who had lived through some of the worst days of the Depression. Many people who lived through the Depression were reluctant to part with goods that they may need when the next "depression" in the economy hit. Thus, my mother- and father-in-law had a treasure trove of artifacts that I could bring in and share with my students. For example, I was able to bring in a clothes iron and a hair curling iron that look somewhat like the same appliances today, with one major exception. Neither had an electrical cord attached to it. As I passed the items around, students were immediately struck by this observation, and we were able to launch into a discussion of the lack of electricity, especially for people who did not live in cities. Electrification of rural areas did not occur until the mid-1930s under the New Deal. My students and I talked about the New Deal; read letters from my mother-in-law's brothers, who were forced to leave the family farm as teenagers because the family could no longer afford to support them; looked at magazine and newspaper advertisements and stories that described life during these desperate times; and sang and analyzed songs such as *Brother Can You Spare a Dime, Happy Days Are Here Again,* and all the great Woody Guthrie songs such as *Roll on Columbia, Roll on.* Of course, we were also able to really dig into *No Promises in the Wind* and *Out of the Dust* (Hesse, 1997), and many other wonderful books that took place during the desperate 1920s and 1930s. We also made and tasted foods that people made in order to survive (e.g., soup made from ketchup and hot water). The touching and talking and questioning about these various artifacts, along with my own explanation of the Great Depression, helped students develop a basic understanding of this time period in American history and allowed them to make better sense of the events they read about in the fiction and nonfiction pieces we subsequently read.

Anything teachers can do to build and activate students' background knowledge on topics that will be encountered in reading will certainly pay comprehension dividends later. Without background knowledge on a topic, it is very difficult to make meaningful headway into what we read.

Comprehension Strategies

Having background knowledge, however, is just a beginning when it comes to developing students' comprehension. Once you have that background knowledge, you have to do something with it to connect with the actual text—these are the various comprehension strategies that we present in this next section.

22
....

CHAPTER 2

*Instructional
Strategies for
Teaching Reading
Comprehension*

Imagery

Have you ever read a book and then seen the movie based on the book? Which did you like better? More often than not, people will choose the book. The reason is that when reading the book, most readers will create a "movie" in their heads; that is, they will create images that correspond to their understanding of the book much more closely than what any Hollywood director might do. Your own personal movie inside your head is just the way you want it to be; hence, you like your version better.

This ability to create mental images while reading is a powerful comprehension strategy. When making these mental images, a reader uses his or her own personal background knowledge to add information that goes beyond the information presented in the text itself. How can teachers make imagery work in their own classrooms?

Connect to Read-Aloud. Perhaps one of the easiest ways to use imagery in the classroom is to use it in conjunction with the read-aloud experience. When reading to your students, ask them to make mental images in their heads while listening to you read—ask them to think about the pictures they may see, but also the smells, the sounds, and the feelings that are part of the images. Then, from time to time stop and ask students to share their images with a group of classmates. Be sure to share your own images, but once you've done it a couple times, share your images last, as they may influence students' own images. When sharing a picture book with students, or a book that contains illustrations, don't share the illustrations until students have created their own internal illustrations. Then talk about how the students' images are different from one another and different from the book illustrator's images.

You may also want to have students make brief sketches while listening to you and then share those sketches with classmates. The sketches become interesting points of discussion about the text. Of course, these same activities can also be integrated into students' own reading.

Sketch to Stretch. One of our all-time favorite imagery strategies, called Sketch to Stretch, takes the previous activity to another level. After students create a sketch from something read or read to them, students share their sketches with a small group of classmates. But rather than explaining his or her own sketch, the student asks his or her classmates to interpret, comment on, and question the sketch.

After the classmates share their insights, the student illustrator provides his or her own explanations for the sketch. Then, the routine continues with the next student sharing his or her sketch in much the same way. This is a terrific way to encourage students to engage in deep, inferential, and interpretive discussions of text and images.

Compare and Contrast

People may not be aware of it, but they often learn (or teach) new things by comparing what is to be learned with something they already know. Not long ago, I (Tim) found myself explaining my role as a college professor to first- and second-graders by comparing it to the students' teachers. I have also heard the Iraq War explained by comparing it to the Vietnam War. And, earlier in my life, I remember the Vietnam War explained in terms of the Korean War and World War II. In my own professional life, I have often used the process of learning to drive a car as an analogy to help teachers understand reading fluency. Just think of all the times that people use the word *like* in their explanations or teachings to others. People often set up an analogy or metaphorical relationship with something they want others to learn and then, through a process of comparing and contrasting what is new to what is already known, people lead themselves and others to deeper understandings of that which is new. Again, as with imagery, this process of comparing and contrasting is employed so frequently that people are often unaware that they are even doing it. But good readers (and teachers) compare and contrast all the time.

In this section we offer some ideas and strategies for using compare and contrast to help students use this technique as a reading comprehension strategy. Harvey and Goudvis (2000) call this strategy *making connections;* the first two strategies we describe come from their book *Strategies That Work.*

Text-to-Self Connections. When reading, a person often will come across something that reminds him or her of something from personal experience or memory. It may be a character that reminds someone of herself or a family member or acquaintance. It may be an episode or problem that was very similar in nature to one that the reader experienced himself. These are text-to-self (TS) connections, and when one lays that book or newspaper article down to reflect on how the read-about experience relates to one's own life's events, then that reader is moving to an ever-deeper level of understanding.

24
....

CHAPTER 2

*Instructional
Strategies for
Teaching Reading
Comprehension*

Making TS connections helps teachers lead students to deeper levels of comprehension, and therefore the strategy should be taught. The easiest way to teach TS connections is for you, the teacher, to make students aware of them by talking about them and modeling how you form them on your own during a read-aloud. Then, through a gradual release of responsibility, you have students making their own TS connections.

While students are reading (or are being read to), stop at strategic spots and ask them think and jot on paper their own TS connections. Have students share with one other. You may wish to list the TS connections for further analysis.

Not all TS connections foster deeper comprehension. Younger students in particular are adept at making connections that are tangential or superficially connected to the text (they may read about a minor character in a book such as a dog and call out a TS connection that they have a dog at home). Be aware that not all connections are strong ones and move students toward an understanding of what makes for good connections. What do you think makes for a good TS connection? We think that the best TS connections are ones that deal with an important part of the text and that lead the reader to deeper analysis of that part through a compare and contrasting with his or her own personal connection.

Text-to-Text Connections.   When something in a book or reading passage reminds you of a character, setting, event, problem, or theme from or author of another book or passage you have read, you have made a text-to-text (TT) connection. As you read with your students, keep in mind other material read in the past and how that the new material may have a connection or relationship with previously read text. You may specifically ask students to make a TT connection with a specific text that you know offers the potential to make good connections. As students become adept at this process, they will surprise you by making connections even you had not thought of. That is when you can take pride in the fact that your students are making good progress in actively involving themselves in constructing meaning as they read.

As with TS connections, the simple process of becoming aware of the relationship or connection is only the start of the process. You want students to become aware of what makes for a good connection and then to use that connection for comparison and contrast—How is this text like and how is it different from a text I have read in the past? Often, the process of making and processing connections is done through conversation and discussion with students. However, you can make the process more formal by providing Venn diagrams and other comparison charts (see sample Inquiry Chart on next page) that allow students to list and analyze similarities and differences (and then synthesize that analysis through a written summary) in the material they are comparing.

Text-to-World Connections.   Often the connection people make is not to something they have personally experienced or read, but to something that they know as part of their background or prior knowledge. These are called text-to-world (TW) connections. When I began thinking about the Iraq War in terms of the Vietnam War, the connections I was making were not based on any one book I had read on the subject, and they weren't based on any particular event in my life, even though I have lived through both wars and have had personal experiences related to each. Rather, the connections I made were more general in nature, based on my reading and personal experiences, but also my interactions with others—some who shared my own opinions about the wars and some who disagreed with me, my television viewing and radio listening, and other things that have shaped my own background knowledge about both wars.

As you can see, making any sort of connection with material a person is currently reading involves background knowledge—in the form of personal experience, other texts read, or general background. However, TW connections are particularly dependent on general background knowledge, and this is where students who have an extensive pool of background knowledge have a huge advantage over those students whose background knowledge is limited. If students do not have sufficient background knowledge on a particular topic, it is difficult to establish a connection to the text being read. Without a connection, the ability to compare and contrast is severely limited.

Individual Texts.   Compare and contrast is a form of informational or exposition writing. Authors often write to inform others by creating a compare-and-contrast format for their text. Interestingly, however, we have noticed that there are many literary texts available that tap into the compare-and-contrast format. Some of our favorites include Paul Fleischman's *Bull Run*, in which he compares and contrasts various characters from the first great battle of the Civil War; *The Pain and the Great One* by Judy Blume, in which sibling rivalry is compared; Remy Charlip's *Fortunately-Unfortunately* looks at the good and not so good side of life's events; and Mary Ann Hoberman's *You Read to Me and I'll Read to You* is a terrific collection of poems for two voices, several of which provide interesting comparisons of

Inquiry Chart

Topic: _____ _____ _____	Question 1: _____ _____	Question 2: _____ _____	Question 3: _____ _____	Question 4: _____ _____	Other Interesting Facts and Figures Found	New Questions
What I know about the topic:						
Source 1:						
Source 2:						
Source 3:						
Synthesis:						

Source: Adapted from Hoffman (1992).

26

characters. My (Tim's) all-time favorite compare-and-contrast trade book, however, is poet's Donald Hall's (1994) *I am the Dog, I am the Cat*. This delightful book compares and contrasts the life of a dog and a cat that live in the same household.

Not only do these wonderful books provide great opportunities to discuss the nature of compare-and-contrast analysis, they also can serve as strong models for students' own compare-and-contrast writing. After reading these books, students will often write their own innovative versions, using other characters, objects, or events that they wish to compare. For example, *I am the Dog, I am the Cat* has morphed into *I am a Book, I am a Computer; I am a Frog, I am a Reptile; I am Ohio, I am Pennsylvania; I am Beverly Clearly, I am Barbara Park; I am a Democrat, I am a Republican; I am a Solid, I am a Liquid;* and *I am Lincoln, I am Washington*. Students love the opportunity to use other writing as a model for their own writing, and when the writing they use as a model is a form of compare and contrast, students also practice the strategy of making meaning by compare and contrast.

Thematic Text Collections.   Teachers have used thematic units and thematic book collections for years as a way to lead students to in-depth and diverse understandings of a particular theme or topic. With a diverse set of materials focused on a particular topic, students have the opportunity to enlarge their background on a particular topic and also to examine a theme or topic from a variety of different genres and perspectives (beyond the disembodied and disinterested perspective taken by most textbooks).

We love the idea of thematic text collections for the opportunities to learn about a topic in great depth. We also think that thematic text collections offer superb opportunities to nurture students' compare-and-contrastive analyses. Although the texts in a collection may share a particular theme or topic, they are often written differently. They may be written in different genre (poetry vs. narrative); different perspective; different emphasis; or different style, artwork, or mood. And it is these differences that are natural fodder for students to engage in compare and contrast.

We love to have students take a pair (or more) of texts from a collection and engage in an analysis of the texts or some features of the text. The use of a compare-and-contrast chart (discussed next) facilitates this analysis and leads students to deeper comprehension, critical analysis, and often new insights. Teachers need to take advantage of what they already have and do to facilitate learning, and this is a particularly potent way to use text collections you may already have to refine this important comprehension strategy.

Compare-and-Contrast Charts. At times, the comparison and contrast that you want students to engage in involves multiple dimensions and/or multiple texts. This more sophisticated comparison and contrast can be put into play through the use *compare-and-contrast charts*. Rasinski and Padak (2004) describe a compare-and-contrast chart as simply a large grid where along one axis texts to be compared and contrasted are listed. The books can share a theme, topic, author, or some other common general thread that ties them together. On the other axis are the features or characteristics against which the various texts are compared. In the example of the comparison-and-contrast chart, the teacher and students have listed on the horizontal axis a set of books by William Steig that they have read. On the vertical axis they have brainstormed a list of characteristics that the class thinks are worth considering. They seem to be elements that have shown up in at least one of Mr. Steig's books. Now, on their own in small groups, the students will engage in analyzing (comparing and contrasting) the books by completing the chart. They will fill in the various boxes with answers to the questions and examples that support their responses. Later, students will complete their analysis by writing a summary that is based on the findings of their analysis and written on the chart.

Compare and Contrast of William Steig Books

	Amos and Boris	Dr. Desoto	Sylvester and the Magic Pebble	Caleb and Kate
Characters (animals or human?)				
Time period (duration of the story?)				
Does a transformation occur?				
Use of alliteration?				

Metaphors.   Metaphors are often taught in English classrooms as a figure of speech or literary device authors use to make for more interesting writing. Moreover, metaphors are usually defined as a kind of implied comparison or description that does not use the word *like*, such as "She was a rock as she stood in front of her accusers" or "He deflated under the ceaseless barrage of insults." Conventional wisdom suggests that metaphors are important in reading because if a reader fails to understand a metaphor, he or she will have difficulty understanding the sentence or passage. Although these may be accurate descriptions of metaphor, we think there is much more to metaphor and metaphorical thinking that can be applied to comprehension and meaning making.

We think of metaphors, like analogies, as a vehicle that invites compare and contrast. How was she really like and unlike a rock as she faced her accusers? What does it mean when it says he deflated? Did he fall down? Did he collapse? Get short of breath?

When students are confronted with metaphors (and analogies) in their reading, they should have the opportunity to explore, usually though compare and contrast, the metaphorical relationship and how it applies and doesn't apply to the actual text. Such analysis moves students into inferential or implied meanings in words, phrases, and passages. Teachers should take time to ask students how the word *rock* actually applies to a woman facing her accuser, and what the word *deflate* has to do with a man facing ridicule.

In addition to analysis of metaphors, we love the idea of having students create metaphors in response to their reading. This can be as simple as having students choose an animal, or an object found in a home or car, and using that object as a metaphor for a character or scene in a passage. How is a particular character like or unlike a broom, a television, a steering wheel? Then, students describe that metaphor in a written paragraph. Similarly, students can choose their own metaphor that best describes a character, scene, or theme of a passage. A comparison of various chosen metaphors can be interesting and insightful.

Metaphors are powerful tools for writing and understanding what is written. More than that, however, the use of metaphors can often open up new insights for readers.

Hypothesis Generation and Testing—Prediction

Human beings seem to have a natural tendency and predilection to predict, hypothesize, or make educated guesses about what they do not know or what will happen in the future. Go to Las Vegas or Wall Street or any race track or bingo hall around the country and you will be surrounded by people who look to the future. Not only in stocks and gambling do people make educated (and sometimes uneducated) guesses, but all endeavors of life seem to invite speculation— from scientists making hypotheses about their next experiment to Hollywood moguls who create the "coming attraction" segments in theaters that whet movie-goers' appetites for the coming movies.

Even readers find themselves constantly speculating about what may happen next in a text. As with the other strategies mentioned, you may not be aware of it as you read, but we can pretty much guarantee that if you are a good reader and a good comprehender, you are constantly looking ahead and making guesses about what you have not yet read. Usually the only time you do become aware of your predictions is when you are surprised by something you did not anticipate in a text. Being surprised is evidence that you did make a prediction, because a surprise is nothing more than making a prediction and finding out that the prediction was incorrect. A reader can never be surprised unless he or she firsts makes a prediction. Consider the following sentence:

"Oh Marcia, I missed you," Bill cried.

Did you make a mental image for the sentence? Perhaps you see two lovers embracing after a long absence. Now look at the sentence that follows the first one:

"Then he aimed and fired again! And this time he didn't miss!"

Was this last sentence what you were expecting to read after having read the initial sentence? Probably not. It is usually after such surprises that a reader becomes aware of this almost natural ability (and perhaps need) to look forward into the future.

Where do predictions come from? They come from the active involvement of the brain using the limited information learned from the text and mixing it with prior knowledge about people and events. This results in making plausible predictions about what will happen in the future in the text.

Although making predictions seems natural and effortless, it is a skill and strategy that is developed through practice. Teachers need to teach this reading comprehension strategy to their students. In the following portions of this section we present a variety of prediction strategies that are easy to implement.

Stop and Predict.   Perhaps the easiest way to encourage predictions is through stopping at strategic parts in a passage that students read or are having read to them and asking them to speculate on what may happen next in the passage and then to explain how they came to that prediction or conclusion—in other words, to explain their reasoning.

Stop and predict can occur after sharing the title, doing a brief picture tour of a book, looking over the outline of a chapter, identifying the author, reading the first paragraph or two, or a chapter, or combining other bits of information that students can use as clues. You might list the predictions on the chalkboard and then adjust the predictions at various stopping points throughout the story. What predictions can be eliminated, what predictions can be added, and what predictions need to be altered?

Russell Stauffer (1980) developed a prediction strategy called the *Directed Reading-Thinking Activity (DR-TA)* as an alternative to the Directed Reading Activity (DRA) lesson format that dominated most reading instruction in the twentieth century. In the more traditional DRA, students passively listened to the presentation of vocabulary and background information about a reading and then responded to questions posed to them by the book author and teacher. Stauffer recognized the need for greater active involvement by the reader and what the reader brought to the task of reading. In the DR-TA, students make predictions about the content of a story or other text based on the title, illustrations, and a limited amount of text presented, as well as the background knowledge that the reader brings to the task. Then, at predetermined stopping points throughout the text, the teacher and students discuss the text in relation to the predictions that were previously generated, with the teacher accepting students' responses but challenging them to justify their responses through the reasoning process that involves their own background knowledge. If reading is a form of thinking, DR-TA truly challenges students to use their thinking skills to make meaning.

Prevoke.   Predictions are made on the basis of a limited amount of information presented to the predictor. In the Stop and Predict and DR-TA, the information is limited by the text that is not yet read. In Prevoke, students are simply presented with a set of words preselected from the text. They use those words to try to come up with a plausible story that anticipates the actual text to be read.

Prevoke is similar to other strategies called Word Splash, Story Impressions, and Vocab-O-Gram. We like the term *prevoke*, as it combines the idea of predictions *(pre)* based on vocabulary *(voke)*. Moreover, the word sounds provocative or stimulating. We certainly think that Prevoke is stimulating comprehension activity. There are three basic steps to Prevoke:

1. *Present words to students.* Select 10 to 15 words that you think are key to the understanding of a particular story. Present the words in the order of their appearance to the students. Quickly go over the words with the students, paying particular attention to the meanings of words with which students may not be familiar. Be sure to use some of the strategies described in *Evidence-Based Instruction in Reading: A Professional Development Guide to Vocabulary* in this series of textbooks.

2. *Organize the words.* Have the students organize the words according to some characteristics that you may provide for them. For example, you could ask students to sort the words around the main features of a story or narrative—what words suggest a time, place, characters, problem, and resolution of the problem. You might also have students sort words according to the feelings they evoke—what words provide a powerful or strong evocation? What words tend to be weak in the feelings evoked? Other categories work well, too.

   As students sort the words, point out that there are no incorrect answers. What you are looking for is not correct answers but good thinking. When students share how they categorized the words, they should also share their reasoning for a particular way of sorting.

   An alternative scheme is to have students sort the words into their own categories. Here, you want students to describe their categories and how they came with up with those categories.

3. *Ask students to predict what the story may be about using the words and knowledge of their ordering as clues.* I often call this step "Playing Sherlock Holmes" (the man who often solved mysteries by reasoning with a limited set of clues; in this case, the clues are the words selected by the teacher).

   Ask students to work individually or in small groups and write their prediction out in the form of a summary statement in which the only the main ideas of the prediction are presented. Predictions are shared prior to the reading with the class. The teacher and students often marvel at the wide diversity of predictions.

The predictions hardly ever capture the essence of the story— but that is not the point. What you are looking for here is active student engagement in constructing meaning, using the words from the text and their own background knowledge. Comprehension is the process of constructing meaning—literal and inferred, and that is exactly what students are doing in Prevoke. The entire three-step process can take fewer than 30 minutes.

There are other forms of the Prevoke process. In Pre-sent, students are given a set of important sentences from a passage and they go through much the same process as in Prevoke to construct plausible predictions about the text. Similarly, in Pre-pict, students make predictions from a given set of illustrations.

Possible Sentences.   Prevoke seems to work particularly well with narrative or story texts. It does not work as well with informational texts, as such texts do not have the same structure. Possible Sentences (Moore & Moore, 1986), a prediction strategy that is particularly well suited for informational texts, has been shown to have a positive effect on students' comprehension (Stahl & Kapinus, 1991).

Like Prevoke, Possible Sentences begins with the selection of 10 to 15 words from an informational passage that students will be reading. About half the words should be well known to students; the other half may require some introduction and explanation by the teacher. Once the words are introduced, the teacher invites students to create five or more sentences they think they may encounter in the text to be read. Each sentence must contain at least two words from the word list. Students' sentences may or may not be accurate statements, but they do reflect something that is possible—hence the name, Possible Sentences. So, for example, preceding a lesson and reading in health science, students were presented with these words from a health unit: *polio, infection, bacteria, virus, incurable, vaccine,* and *Lyme disease.* Students came up with the following sentences:

1. Lyme disease causes polio.
2. Polio is an incurable disease.
3. A virus causes polio.
4. Only bacteria cause infections.

Two of these sentences are true. But that does not matter. The goal is to actively engage students in processing the words, using their background knowledge as much as possible, to make hypothetical statements, and constructing meaning. And the students are doing so with these possible sentences.

34
....

CHAPTER 2

*Instructional
Strategies for
Teaching Reading
Comprehension*

Students present and discuss their various hypotheses to their classmates. Sentences that are clearly true or untrue are identified immediately. The unknown statements are the ones the teacher has the students focus on in their reading. Students read the passage with the purpose of trying to verify or reject the sentences that they were not sure about. From the preceding list, students were able to come to consensus that sentences 1 and 4 were false. They were rewritten to reflect true information.

1. Lyme disease does not cause polio.
4. Bacteria and viruses can cause infections.

Students were less sure about sentences 2 and 3, and so they read the passage in order to try to check on those statements.

After reading the passage, students return to the unverified statements and discuss the passage from the point of view of accepting or rejecting the sentences. Essentially these statements take the place of the questions that are normally found at the end of each chapter of an information book. The big difference, however, is that students generated the questions—and all teachers know that students are more likely to engage themselves in a reading if they are guided and inspired by their own wonderings and ideas about a topic, rather than by the questions that a teacher or a textbook author asks.

The sentences that are verified as true are marked as true. The ones that are identified as false are rewritten to be true. From the previous example, students were able to reject sentence 2 and accept sentence 3. Sentence 2 was rewritten in this way:

2. Vaccinations can prevent a person from getting polio.

These verified and rewritten sentences reflect students' new learning. Students find it exciting to see the fruits of their own research and reading displayed on the chalkboard.

Question Asking and Answering

For many years, teachers used class discussions, usually in the form of question asking by the teacher (usually low-level literal questions) and question answering by students, as a central strategy for teaching comprehension. The research review findings of the National Reading Panel (2000) found that teachers were at least partially on the right track—questioning is a way to guide readers into making sense of what they read. Not only is the responding to questions good for comprehension, but the asking of questions also facilitates comprehension. For a student to come up with a good question on a topic or text, he or she really has to think deeply about the meaning of that passage.

The problem with questioning in the traditional format was the nature and type of questioning. The discussions that teachers had with students were not the kind of discussions that you might find in an adult book club, where participants ask meaningful questions for which they do not know the answer. In the traditional school approach to discussion, only the teacher asked the questions, and most of the questions were low-level factual questions that required a word or two in response and that could easily be found and checked from only the text itself. And, of course, the teacher already knew the answers of the questions (if he or she didn't know the answers, they were printed in the teacher's edition of the basal reader).

Although questioning is good, it is important to examine the nature of the process to make questioning work well for students. Here are some key principles for questioning:

- Questioning should be an authentic task that takes place in an authentic discussion format.

- Questions should be asked by both teachers and students.

- Questions should be ones that the person asking the question does not necessarily know the answer in advance or ones for which there is no correct answer.

- Questions asked should be higher-level questions that require the person asking and responding to use not only the information presented on the page but also his or her own background knowledge and reasoning skills. Answers do not necessarily have to be correct, but should be thoughtful and reasonable. Such questions may begin with "I wonder . . . ?" "What do you think about . . . ?" "If this were to happen, what . . . ?" "Why do you think . . . ? "What caused . . . ?"

So, although questioning is a great strategy for fostering deeper understanding of texts, teachers need to think more about how to develop good questions and how to answer questions in thoughtful and intelligent ways.

How do teachers do this? We return to the Gradual Release of Responsibility Model presented in Chapter 1 to provide the framework for using questions. Teachers must talk about questions with students: Why are questions important? What kinds of questions are the best kind to ask? What do good questions look like? This can be done by modeling for students with what is often called a *think-aloud technique*. Teachers simply allow their thinking to bubble to the surface of visibility, through their own language, so that students can see (hear) what is happening inside the teacher's head when she or he devises questions. If teachers do not make this thinking process apparent to students, how else can they see (hear) the process of devising good questions? Although it may at first seem awkward for the teacher to do this, it really becomes quite easy with practice—the teacher is simply adding volume to the thoughts in his or her head. Teaching is the process of making visible that which is normally invisible for students.

Later, the teacher asks students to practice the same process on their own, perhaps guiding them in a step-by-step fashion. Ask students first to think of and share with one another an "I wonder . . ." question, then a "What do you think . . . ?" question, and then other questions that are initially modeled by the teacher.

Finally, the teacher may ask students to come up with their own questions and to share them with the class. Throughout this process, students are asked to respond to the questions in their own ways. Knowing that there are no necessarily correct answers for higher-level inferential and critical-level questions, teachers (and students) need to be accepting of students' responses but also guide students to even more sophisticated wonderings and questions.

In the previous section of this chapter we discussed the role of predictions in comprehension. A prediction can easily be restated as a question. A prediction statement such as, "In the next part of the story, Caleb will make himself known to his wife, Kate" could easily be restated as a question, "I wonder if Caleb will ever be able to get Kate to recognize that he is really her husband?" All the strategies we have mentioned earlier as well as the ones we will be presenting later in this chapter have much in common. Essentially, they all attempt to get readers to use their own existing knowledge, along with the information taken from the text itself, to construct new meanings and understandings that go beyond both what the reader already knows and what the text is presenting.

Summarizing, Synthesizing, and Written Response to Reading

Traditional notions of reading comprehension associated comprehension with the ability to simply recall information that had been encountered in print. Although the ability to take in and then recall textual information may be a part of comprehension, it is a rather small and low-level part. For us, comprehension means identifying the important parts of what has been read and then doing something with that information—transforming it into something that is different from what had been initially read.

That conceptualization of reading comprehension first assumes an ability to prioritize or identify the major elements of a text. This is what summarizing is all about—succinctly identifying the key pieces of information in a text. Summarizing can be done orally and it can be done in writing. Both are important. However, we wish to give added importance to written summarization because it forces readers to respond in a form similar to the way the initial text was written. The process of writing a summary forces the writer to slow down his or her thinking and become more reflective and thoughtful toward the text.

Although most teachers have a good idea of what a summary is, understanding how to go about developing one is a bit more complex. Again, it is a process that is invisible as it takes place inside one's head. Writing a summary does make the process a bit more visible for students. Although summarizing is a somewhat idiosyncratic task and each person has his or her own ways of doing it, there are some general steps that can help students see how to develop a summary.

1. Take notes as you read a passage. Try to identify key bits of information. Try to state the information in your own words.

2. Look over the notes and decide what is not necessary. Delete information that is either unimportant to the overall idea of the passage or that is too specific—information that is covered in other notes.

3. Organize the remaining notes into logical groups. Find a note or make new notes that identify or describe the category or group.

4. Write a summary of the passage you read; aim at telling the main points of the passage you have read and using your notes to tell the story of the passage.

This process is one that lends itself very well to the gradual release of responsibility. Students need to see their teacher struggle to make sense of reading over and over again. Then they need to practice the skill on their own under the guidance of their teacher.

One trade book we particularly like for learning to summarize is *The Important Book* by Margaret Wise Brown (1990). In this classic book, Brown describes in a summary paragraph everyday objects and items such a spoons, shoes, and apples. Each paragraph begins with a statement of the important thing about a particular object (main idea). This is followed by a list of other key characteristics, and then the page concludes with a restatement of the first sentence, the important thing about the focal item. Each page, then, provides students with a wonderful example of a summary paragraph—the main idea followed by supporting details and concluded with a restatement of the main idea. We use it regularly to help students internalize the components of a summary.

Synthesizing—Summarizing across Multiple Sources

Synthesizing takes summarizing to the next level. One normally thinks of summarizing as finding the main ideas of the text. Synthesizing involves finding the main ideas from several texts and other sources, including the readers' own prior knowledge, and combining those ideas into a larger summary. Writing an "important" passage about all the entries in *The Important Book* (Brown, 1990) is an example of a synthesis of the multiple passages that Margaret Wise Brown created.

The process we outlined earlier is the same process we recommend for creating a synthesis. Determine the main ideas from a variety of sources, organize them in some logical fashion, and then write them up as a summary—a sort of summary of summaries.

The graphic organizer shown earlier in this chapter, adapted from Hoffman (1992), provides a guide for readers in using multiple sources to create a synthesis. A student begins with a topic and brainstorms questions he or she would like to answer about the topic. Then the student identifies what he or she already knows about the questions as well as other interesting information. Next, the student finds other sources of information, including texts, and summarizes information from these sources that pertain to the guiding questions as well as other interesting information not related to the questions.

From the various sources, the student then responds to each question by writing a synthesis based on the various summaries and personal knowledge on the topic. All this investigation may lead to other interesting questions to pursue at a later time. Finally, with all the questions, summaries, and syntheses organized on the inquiry chart, the student is now able to write a research report that is, in effect, a synthesis of the information she or he has collected. The inquiry chart provides an effective map of how to go about doing an in-depth and multisource investigation of a topic. Indeed, we find that we use something like an inquiry chart in our own studies and investigations. The inquiry chart provides the scaffold that allows teachers to guide students' own inquiry. Later, as responsibility is gradually released to students, they can use the inquiry chart on their own or adapt it to their own style of inquiry.

Beyond Summaries—Transformational Writing.   Summaries and syntheses are not the only way a reader can respond in writing to something that has been read. In fact, we believe there is a higher level of written response that goes beyond the summary. A summary stays close to the information in the text. Transforming the text into a new written form requires an even higher form of thinking and comprehension. I (Tim) use food preparation as a metaphor to help understand and describe this idea. When I am really hungry, I might grab an apple and eat it. That requires very little understanding of the apple. My wife is more likely to take an apple, peel it, core it, and slice it into bite-sized pieces. In essence, she is summarizing that apple by distilling it to its important (and most edible) parts. When she wants to be really creative, she cuts up that apple as well as an orange, some strawberries, a banana, perhaps a peach, throws in some walnuts, and mixes in some low-fat yogurt to make a delicious fruit salad. She has transformed that apple (and other ingredients) into something beyond what it was originally. What process demonstrates the greatest understanding of the apple? Arguably, the last process of transforming the fruit into something more than the original requires the greatest understanding of the apple.

In a similar sense, transforming texts that are read into some other written form requires the reader to dive deep into meaning and interpretation of the original text. When students turn the content of a story into a script, a poem, an advertisement, a monologue, or a dialogue, they have to access the deep meaning of the text and then restate it in another form. What are some of the forms that students can use to transform a text? The list is long—here are just a few:

- One of many forms of poetry
- A script performed as Readers' Theater
- A song lyric
- A speech, monologue, or dialogue from various characters
- A personal letter or journal entry
- A letter to the editor of a newspaper
- A script for a television advertisement
- An advice column
- An obituary or epilogue
- A prequel or sequel to the original story
- A rewrite of the story but
  —Changing the gender of the characters
  —Changing the point of view of the text
  —Changing the setting—time or place

What other forms of written response can you think of?

Have you ever read or experienced something that required you to respond in some way? Perhaps you had to talk it through with a friend or spouse, maybe you wrote a letter of complaint, or perhaps you simply made an entry into your personal journal. Each of those responses required you to think through the passage or experience a bit more reflectively than you might otherwise have done. That thoughtful reflection is the process of understanding or comprehension that we want all our students to engage in.

Nonlinguistic Response to Reading

Written response is a wonderful way to move students toward deeper meaning. Oral response in the form of group or partner conversation or discussion serves the same purpose. If you subscribe to Howard Gardner's (2000) theory of multiple intelligences, you know that there are other ways to think about and understand the world—ways that do not require language. We believe that opportunities for students to respond to what they read in ways that do not necessarily require written or oral language can also help readers dive deeper into meaning. This may be especially true for those students who are more gifted in areas other than language, such as spatial awareness, visualization, music, and movement. In nonlinguistic forms of response to reading, students are asked to recast the text in ways that do not require language. In the same way as written and oral response, the process of creating a nonlinguistic response requires the reader to dive deep into meaning.

Readers who take an event and recast it as a visual image are interpreting the text meaningfully, but in a form different from the original. Similarly, when another reader finds or creates a piece of music that seems to reflect the meaning of a passage, he or she is processing that passage meaningfully, making meaning. Asking students to respond nonlinguistically to passages they read is, in effect, asking them to comprehend what they have read in a different way, on a different plane. Yet, despite the form, comprehension is still occurring.

Here are a few ways students can respond to what they read in a nonlinguistic manner:

- *Visual response.* Readers respond to their reading by creating a drawing or other form of visual art that represents some meaningful aspect of what they have read. They ask for responses from their classmates to what they have created before sharing their own interpretation of their work. Students may also find visual art that represents the meaning of a text at a concrete (e.g., Leutze's *Washington's Crossing the Delaware*) or abstract (Picasso's *Guernica*) level.

- *Graphic response.* In graphic response, readers recast the information from the text, or some portion of the information, as a chart, table, graph, map, schedule, time line, or other form of graphic display. Readers, for example, can create a map that reflects the movements of characters or scenes in a story. They can create a table that reflects a quantitative analysis of events in a story, such as the number of times a particular word, phrase, or stylistic element occurred within a story.

- *Musical response.* Readers respond to a reading by finding or creating a musical composition that reflects the meaning of the text. A fine example of such a response is Richard Roger's *Victory at Sea*, which was his musical response to the sea battles that took place in the Pacific Ocean during World War II.

- *Culinary response.* If a text lends itself to food and food preparation, students can make dishes that are reflective or symbolic of characters, scenes, events, or themes represented in a passage.

- *Artifact collections.* Artifact collections, jackdaws, and minimuseums are effective tools for teachers to help students build background knowledge. An artifact collection can be an

42
....

CHAPTER 2
*Instructional
Strategies for
Teaching Reading
Comprehension*

accumulation of items, made or original, that is central to the understanding of a passage. Alone or in groups, students hunt for, collect, and display items related to a text that was read. Ideally, the items reflect and represent key meanings that are presented in the text.

• *Kinesthetic response.* In kinesthetic responses, students use their bodies and bodily movements to interpret a text. Often, kinesthetic response is combined with language in the form of plays, but it does not always have to be that way. Pantomime allows students to act out a scene or event from a passage without using words.

Another form of kinesthetic response is tableau. In tableau, a reader or group of readers choose a still-life scene or event from a passage and recreate it, using their own bodies as the instruments for portraying the event. In essence, students become statues that represent the meaning of a portion of the scene. Some performers my be characters from the scene; others transform themselves into animals, trees, doors, and objects essential to the scene. When students perform their tableau, the other students in the class are invited to interpret the tableau—to try to guess what the tableau group is performing. It becomes, then, an interpretation of the tableau interpretation—a double inference.

Once students become familiar with tableau, teachers can add to it by tapping performers on the shoulder while they are standing still. Once tapped, the performer can some to life for a few seconds, either uttering a few words in character or making a brief movement that adds depth to the character he or she is performing.

Obviously, these nonlinguistic responses do require language to some degree as students plan, implement, and then respond to their nonlinguistic creations. The nonlinguistic responses, however, are the primary vehicles for leading students into higher levels of comprehension that touch the essential meanings of the texts read and then go well beyond it. Meaning and creative thinking are facilitated through the process.

Story Structure and Graphic Organizers

Have you ever found yourself lost in the middle of an unfamiliar city or on a remote country road? Unless you have one of those global positioning systems in your car, it is very likely that you pulled out a map to reorient yourself to the geography of the place and planned a way to reach your intended destination.

Many people rely on graphic information to negotiate the world they live in, whether a street map, a bus or school schedule, or even a lesson plan book. I know for myself, I am always carrying around in my pocket a list of things I need to do, items I need to buy, or places I need to visit. Graphic information helps people make better sense of what may otherwise be a confusing world.

The same is true for reading. Graphic information can help readers make better sense of the material they are reading. These reading-related maps are called *graphic organizers* or *text maps*. Just as with street maps, these text maps help a reader get the "lay of land" when it comes to the material she or he will be reading. The inquiry chart shown earlier in this chapter is a fine example of how a graphic organizer can help a reader organize and make sense of the material he or she reads.

As we mentioned in Chapter 1, there are several text structures that students encounter when reading. Reading passages have various underlying structures or organizations. Stories or narratives, perhaps the most common form of reading in the early grades, are generally organized in a sequential or chronological manner. Informational text, on the other hand, is usually organized differently—in a hierarchical structure, as an enumeration, in a compare-and-contrast format, or as a cause-effect/problem-solution organization. Having an understanding of the underlying structure of a text can significantly assist a reader's meaningful journey through the text in much the same way that knowledge of the underlying organization of a city's street system can facilitate a traveler's journey through an unfamiliar town.

Like the organization of a city, the structure of a text can usually be portrayed graphically, as a map. And in much the same way that a street map can help a traveler, a text map can help a reader find her or his way through a text. A story map is usually portrayed in a way such as this:

$$A \rightarrow B \rightarrow C \rightarrow D \rightarrow E$$

Event A involves the introduction of the characters and setting. Event B presents the problem, and items C and D involve a development of the problem. The resolution to the story occurs with item E. An informational text may be portrayed this way:

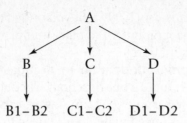

Letter A represents the main idea or thesis of the text—for example, the causes of World War II. Letters B, C, and D represent three particular causes of the war. These may include the economic depression suffered particularly by Germany after World War I, the rise of fascism in Germany and Italy, and perhaps the lack of preparedness of the Allies for the war. Letters B1 and B2 involve further elaboration of letter B. For example, the economic depression suffered in Germany was due to the harsh reparations forced on Germany and the overall economic slump suffered throughout the world in the late 1920s. Similarly, C1, C2, D1, and D2 represent further elaborations of their respective elements.

Writers often write from outlines, maps, or graphic organizers. If teachers can help students read with the underlying organization of the text in mind, teachers will be helping them think like the writers who created the text, and this will lead to improved comprehension. Think of the types of underlying structures that might accompany the following titles:

- The Life of Abraham Lincoln
- Earthquakes: Causes and Consequences
- Scientists Who Changed the World
- Energy Sources
- The Structure of the Atom
- Democracy and Socialism
- My Neighborhood

Many texts may have more than one text structure, with one structure embedded within another. Helping students make it through these complexities can make meaning more transparent for students.

The way to teach comprehension using text structures and text maps is to provide students plenty of exposure to graphic representations of text structures. From as early as possible, show students how passage structure can be portrayed graphically. Begin with narrative and then move gradually into other text forms. At first, you will want to share already completed text maps with the students. Later, provide students with only partially completed text maps, which they will need to complete on their own. Eventually, students will be able to make and explain their own text maps that are created after reading, and will also be able to survey and understand independently completed text maps that are presented to them prior to reading.

Text structure is not the only information that can be presented in graphic form (graphic organizers). In fact, much information in life can and is presented as graphs, tables, charts, diagrams, maps, time lines, schedules, and the like. Many students who have no difficulty comprehending information presented in traditional text formats have difficulty with texts presented in graphic form. Comprehension of graphically portrayed information is a legitimate form of literacy comprehension and needs to be presented and taught to students. Think of all the information that is presented in graphic form. Daily—whether in textbooks, newspapers, the Internet, television, and other sources—information is distilled into and presented as tables, charts, graphs, and other graphic forms.

The way to teach graphic organizers is through in-depth exposure, explanation, and authentic application (making and interpreting graphic organizers) using the gradual release of responsibility model. Find or make graphs and tables and expose them to your students regularly. They can be graphs representing simple ideas, such as gender in a classroom or school, or survey results among students on various items such as favorite foods or authors. Present and explain these graphics to students. Ask questions that students answer by interpreting the graphic organizer (e.g., "After examining the graphic organizer for the food survey, which foods would you serve if you owned a café in our school?"). Can you see working with a different graphic organizer every day of the week? We can.

As time goes on, the organizers become more complex and varied. From simple charts and bar graphs, students work with multivariable tables and line graphs. Moreover, as you release responsibility to students, you ask them to create their own graphic organizer from information that you present to them or that they collected on their own. (At this point in your reading, for example, you may wish to survey members of your study group to determine the number of readers who are finding the information in this chapter useful. Then, determine a way to display that information as a graphic organizer. Various members of your group can share and explain how they chose to present the information and see if other members of the group can interpret the organizer effectively.)

People learn to read and comprehend written text by lots of supportive and supported reading of various forms of written texts. Similarly, graphic organizers are best learned by plenty of supportive and supported exposure to and interpretation of various forms of graphic organizers.

Cooperative Learning

Often, it is thought that reading is primarily an individual task in which the reader encounters the text alone. It certainly seems that way. But in reality, reading is also a social task. It is done with others, especially the response portion of reading. I can hardly read something that delights or angers me without somehow sharing that reading with my wife or another person. I often seek affirmation to my own conclusions, but sometimes find that my respondents, because they have different backgrounds and dispositions that they bring to the text, have interpretations or opinions of the text that are different from my own understanding. Moreover, the response that they share with me challenges my own thinking or helps me see the message in another way. In any case, sharing my reading with another person leads to a deeper understanding of the meaning of the text and a greater appreciation for the different and multiple understandings that others may have from reading the same text. Unless I share my reading with others, I may only be reinforcing my own egocentric view of the world and fail to grow as much I could from hearing others' viewpoints and sharing my viewpoints with them.

The research on group or cooperative learning in general and reading in particular is compelling (National Reading Panel, 2000). People learn best in learning communities. For instance, some of you right now are reading this book as part of a book club, discussion group, or professional development team. People learn more by sharing, challenging, and extending their understandings of their world and their texts.

In our opinion, cooperative learning is not a comprehension strategy as much as it is vehicle for delivering the comprehension strategies that we presented earlier in this chapter. And, in this section, we present some ways of thinking about using cooperative learning as the vehicle for comprehension strategy instruction.

Think Pair Share. Think Pair Share is a generic cooperative learning strategy that involves students in moving from individual thought to shared meaning-making in a reading situation. The process is quite simple. Students read (silently or orally) to a predetermined point in a text. At this point, they are prompted to think individually about some aspect of what has been read (a comment on a character or what is particularly interesting, a curiosity of what will happen next in the passage, an image of what has developed in their minds). Students can jot their responses on paper or keep their thoughts internal. Next, students find a partner and discuss their individual responses, then together create collaborative responses to the original prompt. Finally, the pairs share their responses with the members of the larger group, who are encouraged to comment on the various responses.

The idea of going from individual to group response encourages students to listen, share, and negotiate meaning with others. Think Pair Share is easily adaptable to other structures. Students can group into threes or fours instead of pairs. They can also move from initially sharing in the large group, moving to pairs, and eventually responding individually to the reading and their various levels of sharing that has occurred.

Partner Reading.   In *Evidence-Based Instruction in Reading: A Professional Development Guide to Fluency*, one of the five books in this series, we described how students can pair with others to read together and build reading fluency. This idea of partner reading can also be used as a cooperative learning strategy to build comprehension. In partner reading, students work with a classmate and read together. The reading can take a variety of forms—alternating paragraphs or sentences, reading chorally together, engaging in echo reading, and so on. At prearranged points, students stop to talk about what they have just read—again, this can involve predicting, summarizing, commenting, or using any of the other strategies we have presented in this chapter. Students then continue partner reading until they come to another stopping point.

Fourth-grade teacher Lorraine Griffith uses partner reading in her sustained silent reading (SSR) period. Lorraine feared that many of her students were simply going through the motions during SSR time. To overcome this, she developed a structure to make students responsible to one another. Students read with a partner orally during the 15- to 20-minute reading period. At the end of the period they summarize what they have read and make a commitment to read a certain number of pages of their chosen text at home silently. This arrangement allows Lorraine to use SSR as a starting point to integrate individual and partner reading, oral and silent reading, and home and school reading.

Literature Discussion Groups. Literature discussion groups or literature circles (Daniels, 2002; McMahon & Raphael, 1997; Noe & Johnson, 1999, Rasinski & Padak, 2004) are an attempt to bring into the classroom the same kind of authentic and engaging discussion that occurs in adult book clubs. After reading a common text, students regularly gather into a group to talk about what they have read. Ideally, the discussions are student led; however, the teacher will likely have to scaffold students into doing the discussions on their own. Again, the gradual release of responsibility model provides a format for making discussion groups work. Initially, the teacher may work with adults or a selected group of students to model how a discussion might take place. Later, students take on the discussion under the watchful eye of the teacher who leads the class in a discussion of the experience. Eventually, students will be able to engage in fruitful and lively discussions without the guidance or support of the teacher.

When initiating discussions it may be helpful to assign specific roles to students so that they have a defined task to prepare for as they read. The strategies we presented earlier can help you in making specific tasks for students. Here are some that we think work well:

- *Group leader:* Leads the discussion and encourages participation
- *Summarizer:* Initiates the discussion with a summary of the reading
- *Text-to-life connector:* Shares and discusses text-to-life connections found in the passage
- *Text-to-text connector:* Shares and discusses text-to-text connections
- *Questioner:* Finds and shares interesting questions that emerge from the passage
- *Imagineer:* Leads a discussion of interesting images in the passage
- *Predictor:* Leads discussion about upcoming events in the next section of the text
- *Sentence finder/Word wizard:* Finds and leads a discussion of interesting sentences and words found in the passage

Literature discussion groups are essentially a form of reciprocal teaching, the process in which students become their own teachers. Being teachers, we all know that the highest form of knowledge on a topic is the ability to teach it to others. Putting students in the role of teachers makes them more aware of not only their own learning process but also the learning of others, requiring them to become masters of the content they are covering.

Comprehension Monitoring

Metacognition, metacomprehension, or comprehension monitoring is a strategy that challenges readers to become aware of their own thinking or comprehending processes and to intervene when effective processing of the text is not taking place. In a sense, it is comprehension of your comprehension, or the quality control mechanism in your reading. Perhaps the most common example of comprehension monitoring happens when you read late at night just before going to sleep. If you are really tired, you tend to go blank while reading the text. You are reading the words, but the words are not really connecting to any meaning in your head. You become aware of this happening and go back and reread what you have read, this time trying to be more alert and focused on meaning. Usually the fatigue returns, you go blank again, and after several episodes of becoming aware of your own lack of comprehension, you make the strategic decision to call it a night, put the book away, and go to sleep.

For some readers, this awareness of their own reading process is not as strong as it should be. Students may read the words but not be fully aware that the words are not making sense or that they are confused by the information presented. They simply continue to read without stopping and making adjustments to their reading. As a result, they comprehend poorly.

Teachers need to help students develop this internal quality control mechanism in their reading. As mentioned earlier, it is best to begin by modeling the process for students and here, again, is where the think-aloud technique works well. As you read to students from time to time, try to describe out loud what you are thinking about with regard to the meaning—what strategies you are employing such as imagery, questioning, connecting, or prediction, and what you do when you are not comprehending what you are reading. This helps students conceptualize this monitoring process that is largely invisible to their eyes.

Later, involve students in discussions centered not only on the content of what they have read but also on their processing of the text. What strategies did they use, where did comprehension begin to break down for them, and what did they do about it? Repair strategies are many and should be made explicit to students:

- Ignore the problem and continue reading.
- Look back and reread the previous sentence, paragraph, or page.

50
....

CHAPTER 2

*Instructional
Strategies for
Teaching Reading
Comprehension*

- Look up definitions for challenging words.
- Develop an alternate or tentative hypothesis and continue reading.
- Examine the illustration and other graphically portrayed information.
- Seek help from another knowledgeable person.
- Take a break and return to the text later.

When students become aware of comprehension monitoring and various strategies for overcoming difficulty, they need the opportunity to try the strategies on their own. "Clicks and clunks" provides a vehicle for students to employ and talk about their comprehension monitoring strategies. In clicks and clunks, the teacher asks students to stop reading at designated points in a text. Then they are asked to determine if the message of the passage is clicking for them or if it clunks. If it clunks, students need to employ a repair strategy for making better sense of what they are reading. Talking about and employing comprehension monitoring strategies will help ensure that students will be successful when reading on their own and when reading more challenging materials.

Comprehension Programs and Materials

Methods, materials, and programs for comprehension instruction and practice are many and growing. They range from practice passages and tests that contain comprehension questions, to comprehension games, to strategy posters, to graphic organizers, to passages that invite students to respond to their reading in various ways meant to foster comprehension. In evaluating such materials and programs, we recommend that you focus on the following questions:

- Is the program based on an accurate conception of reading comprehension?
- Is the program (materials and activities) intended for the range of readers that you teach?
- Will children find texts engaging? Do the passages represent a range of genre from which readers can make meaning?
- Is the overall instructional routine appropriate?
- Is attention paid to teacher modeling and a gradual release of responsibility to students?

- Are a variety of scaffolding practices available for children who need it?
- What levels of comprehension are stressed—only literal? Or is inferential and critical comprehension fostered as well?
- Are assessment ideas and activities offered?

Comprehension of what they read may seem to be a natural and effortless activity for many people. But the fact of the matter is that it is an active and complex process in which the reader works to make meaning of what he or she reads. Good readers already know something about what they are reading and they employ a variety of strategies to make meaning from text. It is the job of teachers to help students become aware of these strategies, acquire them through regular and guided practice, and then use them in their own independent reading. Learning to read is too important to leave the learning of these strategies to chance.

As you finish reading this chapter, try employing some of the comprehension strategies that have been presented here. Respond to some of these prompts:

- Did you already know something about comprehension before beginning this chapter? How did that knowledge affect your reading of this chapter?
- What sorts of images do you have or did you create as you read this chapter?
- What do you think the next chapter in this book will be about?
- What questions do you have about comprehension as a result of reading this chapter? Do you know the answers to your questions?
- Are you able to write a summary of this chapter?
- Can you transform the information in this chapter into another form—a dialogue, a script, a letter, a poem?
- Are you able to transform this chapter into a meal (use a meal as a metaphor for the information in the chapter) or a pantomime?
- Could you create a text map for this chapter?
- Can you present this chapter as a table or chart?
- Were there areas of the chapter that you had trouble with? What did you do?
- Can you discuss this chapter with your colleagues (see next section)?

Professional Development Suggestions

ACED: Analysis, Clarification, Extension, Discussion

I. REFLECTION (10 to 15 minutes)

ANALYSIS:

- What, for you, were the most interesting and/or important ideas in this chapter?

  _____

  _____

  _____

  _____

- What information was new to you (or different from your own prior knowledge)?

  _____

  _____

  _____

  _____

CLARIFICATION:

- Did anything surprise you? Confuse you? Cause you to stop and reflect?

  _____

  _____

  _____

  _____

- Was there anything missing from or overlooked in this presentation on reading comprehension strategies?

  _____

  _____

  _____

  _____

EXTENSION:

53
....
CHAPTER 2

*Instructional
Strategies for
Teaching Reading
Comprehension*

- What new questions or wonderings do you have about teaching reading comprehension?

  _____

  _____

  _____

  _____

- Can you relate any information presented in this chapter to your own previous teaching experiences or to students you have taught in the past?

  _____

  _____

  _____

  _____

- What new insights do you have about teaching reading comprehension that you developed as a result of reading this chapter?

  _____

  _____

  _____

  _____

II. DISCUSSION (20 minutes)

- Form groups of 4 to 6 members.

- Appoint a *facilitator (timer)* and *recorder*.

- Share responses. Make sure that each person has shared his or her responses to each category (Analysis/Clarification/Extension).

- Help each other with any areas of confusion.

- Answer and/or discuss questions raised by group members.

54
....

CHAPTER 2

*Instructional
Strategies for
Teaching Reading
Comprehension*

- On chart paper, the recorder should summarize the main discussion points and identify issues or questions the group would like to raise for general discussion.

III. APPLICATION (10 minutes)

- Based on your reflection and discussion, how might you apply what you have learned from this chapter?

_____

_____

_____

_____

CHAPTER 3

Assessing Reading Comprehension

*I*n each of the books in this series, we have identified several "big ideas" to guide your thinking about assessment. These big ideas apply to assessing all aspects of literacy learning (indeed, to all learning), but the comments and examples below frame them in the context of assessing children's comprehension.

• *Focus on critical information.* Aim for a direct connection between what you need to know and the assessment tools/strategies you use. You can decide about critical information by considering the broad definition of comprehension presented earlier in this book in light of your own students. Conventional comprehension assessment focuses on content-based questions related to a text. From a student's response to particular questions about a particular text, you try to make inferences about the student's general comprehension abilities. Although such text-specific information is helpful, keep in mind the National Reading Panel's emphasis on the importance of comprehension strategies. Your assessment plans, then, should include ways to look at students as strategic readers—what they are able to do in addition to what they know. To do this, it may help to think about a student whose comprehension is excellent. Try making a list of his or her observable indicators: What does he or she do? Say? Having thought about the abstract definition and your own students, then, you can decide on critical information. McTighe and Wiggins (2004) suggest that this process works best when it begins at the end: (1) If the desired result is for learners to . . . (2) then assessment should provide you with evidence of . . . (3) and so assessment tasks need to include some things such as . . . .

• *Look for patterns of behavior.* Rob Tierney (1998) notes that assessment "should be viewed as ongoing and suggestive, rather than fixed or definitive" (p. 385). No one instance can possibly tell you what you need to know about a child's comprehension. What affects your own comprehension? The text? The task? Your interest, motivation, or background knowledge? Even environmental factors such a noise level? How about your own ability to concentrate? Do you comprehend as well when you are sleepy or when something else is on your mind? All these factors (and possibly more) also affect your students' comprehension abilities, so your goal should be to find patterns of comprehension behavior. To do this, you need a plan. Get baseline information about children at the beginning of the year. Then select a few children to focus on each week. You can simply identify children to observe using a class list, but you may also want to select children about whom you need more information or children whose current behavior is surprising in some way (Rasinski & Padak, 2004). You might find the chart of Observational Progress

Notes shown on page 67 helpful for this purpose. Short-term, single-instance data can tell you about bigger issues but only if you capture enough single instances to see patterns.

• *Recognize developmental progressions (can't, can sometimes, can always) and children's cultural or linguistic differences.* Tierney (1998) advises that "assessment should be more developmental and sustained than piecemeal and shortsighted" (p. 384). He continues, "I envision . . . assessments that build upon, recognize, and value rather than displace what students have experienced in their worlds" (p. 381). Your plans should be sensitive to both of these issues. With regard to the former, children can (and do) learn to comprehend before they can read independently; what insights can assessments of children's listening comprehension ability provide? You may want to include listening comprehension as a focus in your overall assessment plans. With regard to the latter, consider the possible influences of cultural differences on children's comprehension. Since comprehension is partially dependent on readers' background knowledge and experiences, it may be particularly important to look at cultural differences in this domain.

• *Be parsimonious.* The question: How much assessment information do you need? The answer: Enough to help you make good instructional decisions. One way to conceptualize this quantity-of-information question is to think in terms of three related layers of assessment information.

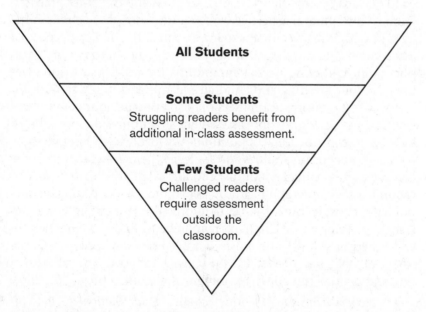

All Students

Some Students
Struggling readers benefit from additional in-class assessment.

A Few Students
Challenged readers require assessment outside the classroom.

Source: Rasinski and Padak (2004, p. 277). Reprinted by permission of Pearson Education, Inc.

At the top of the figure is what is done for and with all students in the class. Begin with a broad plan to assess children's comprehension at the beginning of the year, perhaps using some of the assessment activities listed later in this chapter. Then, perhaps, reassess quarterly. As each assessment cycle concludes, think about results—what (or who) do you still have questions about? This is the point to move to the second layer of the triangle. Here, you will do more focused (and time-consuming) comprehension assessments. You might work individually with a child about whom you have questions. Perhaps an oral retelling will provide the additional information you need, or you may want to assess comprehension with easier text or a different genre. Conversations about comprehension can also prove helpful. You might want to ask the child how she or he tries to think about the author's message while reading or about comprehension "fix-up" strategies. If you still have questions after this additional assessment, don't hesitate to ask for outside help. A child or two in the class may benefit from a diagnosis by a reading specialist or other highly specialized professional. Don't delay and don't hesitate. Every lost day represents lost opportunities for that child's learning. Above all, keep assessments at these different layers related to one another, focused on the same key comprehension issues.

• *Use instructional situations for assessment purposes.* Tierney (1998) notes that, ideally, "assessments should emerge from the classroom rather than be imposed upon it" (p. 375). We can think of two good reasons for this stance, one conceptual and the other practical. From a conceptual perspective, you want to know how children behave in typical instructional situations. After all, a major purpose of assessment is to provide instructional guidance. From a practical standpoint, gathering assessment information from instruction saves time for your teaching and children's learning; children don't learn much of value during testing sessions. To evaluate your comprehension instruction for possible assessment situations, you might begin by listing the instructional opportunities available to children to show their comprehension abilities and strategies. Remember to look at the comprehension process, not just products. Then develop a plan to capture observations about children's comprehension during instruction. Also consider other sources of information; for example, you can learn something about children's comprehension by reading their literature response logs or their lists of books read in school or at home. Above all, take Karen West's (1998) advice to heart: "I want instruction and evaluation to be in meaningful authentic contexts" (p. 550).

• *Include plans for (1) using assessment information to guide instruction and (2) sharing assessment information with children and par-*

ents. The last step of your assessment planning might be to double-check ideas against their primary purposes: to help you teach more effectively and to communicate your insights with children and their parents. With regard to the former, it may be particularly important to think about how you can adjust instruction for children who have comprehension problems. Can you provide easier texts or extra comprehension support for them? Moreover, consider how you can share information about comprehension with children and their parents. Knowing that they are making progress will keep children engaged in their learning. Assessment conversations are also good ways to help children develop more abstract concepts about reading, such as comprehension monitoring. And parents, of course, are both interested in their children's progress in school and frequently willing to assist in their children's education. Rob Tierney (1998) reminds us that it's important to keep parents informed, but more than that, involved: "Rather than keep the parent or caregiver at arm's length . . . , we need to embrace the concerns that parents have and the contributions they can make" (p. 380).

With these general principles of assessment in mind, you need to keep the primary purpose for which you do all assessment in reading: Is your instruction having the desired impact on your students? This is certainly true of reading comprehension. As in the other areas of reading, it is important to ask questions for which assessment provides the answers. Here are a few:

- Is your instruction having an impact on students' learning to understand what they read?
- Are your students progressing adequately in their comprehension development over time?
- If your students are not progressing adequately in comprehension, what areas of comprehension are of greatest concern?

Although a good comprehension assessment program will provide answers to these questions, teachers have the added burden of trying to answer these assessment-related issues in the least amount of time and with the fewest resources, for time and resources given to assessment is time and resources that are taken away from instruction. There is no question that teachers can do an in-depth assessment in reading that will provide a thorough understanding of each student's level of achievement in reading as well as identify each student's particular strengths and weaknesses in reading. However, the cost of doing such an assessment may mean that very little time is available for instruction. Some schools mandate that individual and detailed reading assessments for all students be done two or three times a year. Teachers in these schools complain loudly that they have very little time to make the progress in reading that the assessments are meant to measure.

Assessment in reading comprehension is a particularly daunting task. Assessment in word recognition, fluency, and vocabulary is relatively simple. Students' ability to decode words, understand words, and read with an appropriate level of fluency is fairly transparent—a teacher can see directly if a student can decode a word, do it fluently, or determine the meaning of a word simply by observing the student in the performance of those tasks. Reading comprehension, however, is much more invisible; it happens more inside the head and thus is not easily observed.

On top of this, reading comprehension is multilayered and multifaceted. As we mentioned earlier in this book, comprehension involves reading at literal, inferential, and critical levels. Readers can be good in one level but not another. All levels are important. Reading comprehension occurs in a variety of texts or genres, written at a variety of levels of difficulty. Good readers need to be able to make meaning on a wide range of text materials. Reading comprehension also involves the various strategies that we presented in the previous chapter. Good readers need to be proficient in most, if not all, of these strategies. Finally, reading comprehension is dependent on the other components of reading that have been presented in the other books in this series. Inadequate reading comprehension may be due to problems in word decoding, vocabulary, or reading fluency. Students may have all the appropriate skills and dispositions associated with proficiency in comprehension but may not be able to comprehend the texts they encounter because they are unable to adequately decode the words in the text.

Assessing Your Own Reading Comprehension Assessment

At this point you might want to explore your own thoughts and ideas on comprehension assessment. The chart that follows may help you take a careful look at your current assessment practices in comprehension. To complete the chart, first list all the ways you currently assess students' comprehension in the "Assessment Tool/Strategy" column. Then consider the information each tool or strategy

Critical Aspects: Comprehension

Assessment Tool/Strategy	Provides information on students' retelling and summarizing information from the text	Provides information on students going beyond the literal information in the text	Provides information on students' critical understanding and judgments about the text	Provides information about students' monitoring of their comprehension	Other information

Notes about revisions:

provides about each of the critical aspects by marking the chart: + = excellent source of information; − = some information; (blank) = no information. When the chart is complete, make plans for revision. Are some critical aspects receiving too much/not enough attention? Can some tools/strategies be eliminated or revised? What revisions will enhance your overall assessment strategies?

What did you conclude by analyzing your current strategies for assessing comprehension? Perhaps you are satisfied that you have enough of the right kind of information about your students. If not, you may find some of the following ideas helpful for supplementing your plans.

Approaching Comprehension Assessment

There are many formalized and standardized tests designed to assess reading achievement and comprehension. Although such assessments have strengths and we do not deny their usefulness, they also have certain limitations that concern us. Such assessments are often time consuming and costly. They also usually provide limited information that is useful to teachers to plan instruction. Perhaps, most importantly, they do not require much input or knowledge on the part of teachers. Teachers merely need to know how to administer the assessment, and this is usually accomplished by reading the test manual that provides an administration script to read to students.

We prefer teachers to be knowledgeable about reading and reading comprehension and to empower teachers to use their knowledge to understand students so that they can make informed decisions about how to best teach students. That is why we tend to favor a more informal, teacher-based approach to assessment. Informal approaches may require a bit more work, but they yield so much more in the way of understanding and precise and effective instruction.

As you can see, assessing reading comprehension has the potential to become enormously complex, even for teachers who are steeped in the knowledge of reading instruction and assessment. This chapter provides you with a reasonable approach to assessing reading comprehension—an approach that is sufficiently rigorous to arm you with information you need to make instruction focused on students' needs, but parsimonious enough to make it simple enough for a novice to implement and efficient enough to allow time and resources for instruction. Let's begin with a simple way to determine if students have at least some degree of understanding of what they read.

Retelling

If you want to know what a person knows from reading a text, you would most likely ask what he or she learned or recalled from the reading. That is essentially what is involved in a retelling. You ask students to read a passage and then ask them to tell (retell) you what they remember from the reading. You then judge the quality of their retelling against a descriptive rubric. The key advantages to a retelling procedure are that it is simple and quick to implement, empowers the teacher to make a professional judgment about students' comprehension, and requires little if any advanced preparation in the way of specific questions to ask students. Here are some things to keep in mind when using a retelling procedure to assess comprehension:

- Tell students before they read the text that you will be asking them to recall for you what they remember from the reading when they are finished.

- When students finish reading the passage give them a few seconds to collect their thoughts, remove the text from their view, and ask them to tell you all they can remember from the reading.

- Feel free to prompt students to recall more information when they end their recall or tell you that there is nothing more they can remember. You might say, "Is there anything else you remember from the passage?" and give them a few seconds to recall. You might ask students to give their opinion about the text or any element within it. Or you might ask if reading the text made them think about or connect with anything from their own experiences. The last two prompts allow students to go beyond the text and provide inferences that they might not spontaneously be provide.

The rubric shown on the next page allows you to judge the quality of the retelling. As you can see, the rubric ranges from a score of 1 for a minimal recall to a score of 6 that reflects a comprehensive, logical summary that also goes beyond the text into logical inferences the student might make about the content.

Using the retelling technique and retelling rubrics are not limited to retelling material read by the students. Comprehension can be affected by factors external to the comprehension process. Students may not comprehend due to poor word recognition or poor fluency in reading. Thus, to control for such factors you may wish to have students retell material that you read to them. When the word recognition and fluency load are removed by your reading the text to

Rubric for Informal Retelling Comprehension Assessment

Ask the reader to retell what he or she can remember after having read a short passage. Score against the rubric:

1. Gives minimal recall, if any, of a fact or two from the passage. Facts recalled may or may not be ones of great importance.

2. Recalls a number of unrelated facts of varied importance.

3. Recalls the main idea of the passage with a few supporting details.

4. Recalls the main idea along with a fairly robust set of supporting details.

5. Provides a comprehensive summary of the passage, logically developed and with great detail that includes a statement of the main idea.

6. Provides a comprehensive summary and make inferences that go beyond the text itself. The inference may be in the form of connections to the student's own life, reasonable judgments about the text or characters or items within the text, or logical predictions about events that go beyond the boundaries of the text itself.

students, are they able to provide an adequate retelling of the passage? You may wish to compare students' retellings when they read the text and when the text is read to them. This may give you good information about the extent to which other factors may influence and perhaps inhibit students' understanding of what they read.

Similarly, you may wish to change the mode of the retelling. Perhaps you can have students retell material to one another and have fellow students rate their classmate's retelling. This will help the students listening to the retelling judge what makes for a good summary of a text. You might also wish to have students write their retelling in the form of a written summary. This will serve the instructional purpose of promoting summarizing and will also allow you to make judgments about students' ability to express their understandings about what they read in written form. Fellow students can also be employed to rate the written retellings of their classmates as a way to develop students' awareness of what makes for a good written summary.

Professional Development Extension. The keys to retellings are the protocol and the rubric—the protocol needs to work in the individual teacher's context, and the rubric must be sensitive enough and descriptive enough to allow the user to make informed judgments about the level of meaning students are constructing as they read. We have found that the retelling rubric serves our own purposes well. We recognize, however, that rubrics need to fit the needs and assessment/instructional styles of the users. Our rubric may not fit your own needs. Thus, at this point we invite you to think about developing your own retelling protocol and rubric. What specific procedures are keys to your own assessment style and situation? How many levels of the rubric work for you? How would the various levels of the retelling rubric describe students' performance? Give it a try. The exercise of developing a protocol and rubric will allow you to think more deeply about comprehension assessment and how it may best work for you. You might want to share your ideas with a colleague.

Assessing Students' Use of Specific Comprehension Strategies—Progress Notes

Retelling provides you with a method for assessing the whole of comprehension—it answers the question, To what extent are students gaining meaning from what they read? Retellings can be administered to students regularly and with different text types. They are simple, quick, and, perhaps most important, they rely on your expert opinion to determine students' performance. Retellings, however, do not provide you with information about the precise strategies that students employ to make meaning. In an earlier chapter, we described several comprehension strategies that will help readers make meaning out of what they read—good comprehenders are competent in many comprehension strategies and use them at the appropriate times. Instructionally, it is to your benefit to know what strategies students know, use, and use well. How can you assess students in these various comprehension strategies? Again, we feel that the best instrument for assessing comprehension is the teacher, and the best method for assessing comprehension is informed observation. To that end, we recommend developing a method for regularly observing and assessing students' performance on the various comprehension strategies we deem important. We call our observational system Progress Notes.

The first step in developing an observational system for assessing specific strategy performance is the development of a set of principles and a protocol. Here are some points that you need to consider in your own principles and protocol:

- What strategies will you observe and assess?
- How often will you observe and assess?
- How will you record your observations? Notes? Will you employ a quantitative rating system, or will you use qualitative notes? Or both?
- Will you use a particular form for recording observations?
- When will you record your observations? During class hours? After school?
- What texts will you use? What levels of difficulty? What genre?

As you can see from our sample Observational Progress Notes chart, the observational system can be quite complex and cumbersome. It is important to take sufficient time to plan a system that will work for you. Perhaps you want to limit your observations to only a few specific comprehension strategies at a time; perhaps you want to limit your observations to a certain period of time; or maybe you want to limit your observations to a particular text genre—say, students' reading informational or narrative material. As important as assessment is, it is important to remember to balance it against instruction—time given to assessment is time taken away from instruction. Nevertheless, periodic note taking can provide an ongoing and rather in-depth picture of students' growth in reading comprehension as well as their ongoing instructional needs for further growth. An advantage of Progress Notes is that you can learn a great deal by watching students engaged in instruction. That is, you don't have to stop teaching in order to test.

The Progress Notes system is intended for use by teachers in assessing students' growth in comprehension. However, we also see the system used as a way to promote students' own awareness of their reading comprehension. Think about having students periodically review and comment on their own development in the various reading comprehension strategies. You could have them rate themselves quantitatively in each area, or rank order each strategy, from most to least useful or comfortable or competent. You could also ask students to write their own comments about their growth in specific areas or ask them to cite specific examples of their own use of strategies in their recent reading. At the very least, this sort of reflection will help develop in students that metacognitive awareness of their own reading processes that may challenge them to make adaptations to strengthen their own reading.

Teachers and students can also use the Progress Notes system collaboratively. We see this as perhaps the best use of the system.

Observational Progress Notes

	First Period	Second Period	Third Period	Fourth Period	Comments
Developing background knowledge					
Uses imagery					
Makes connections					
Uses metaphors					
Predicts					
Questions (asks and answers)					
Summarizes					
Creative written response to reading					
Nonlinguistic response to reading					
Text structure and graphic organizers					
Understands and uses graphs, tables, charts, maps, and so on					
Discussion groups and cooperative learning					
Monitors comprehension					

Teachers confer with individual students periodically and use the recording form to guide the discussion and record both the teacher's and the students' observations and comments on the students' reading. A shared assessment of this type will help increase students' metacognitive awareness of reading and at the same time allow the teacher to have a voice in shaping that awareness, making an assessment, and developing plans for future instruction.

Self-Assessment

Students can and should have some say in evaluating their own comprehension growth. In addition to fostering students' sense of responsibility for their own learning, self-assessment invites students to think metacognitively about comprehension, to think about it as an abstract concept. This helps students because it serves as a subtle reminder that readers always strive to make meaning. Ideas for self-assessment include:

- *Occasional conversations.* You might ask students to assess their comprehension ("How well did you understand what the author was saying?") or to discuss comprehension monitoring ("Who got stuck? What did you do to solve this problem? Did it work? How do you know?").
- *Checklists.* You might create simple checklists for students to complete, perhaps using smiley faces as response options. Items on the list could include statements such as "I understood," "I made connections," "I tried to fix when I got stuck," or "I made predictions."
- *Journal entries.* On occasion, ask children to write about comprehension in their journals. Prompts could include some of the statements used in the checklist in the previous paragraph.

Assessment no doubt is a sticky issue. But effective instruction cannot exist without effective assessment. Knowing where students are and what they need is fundamental to making the most of instruction. Key to assessment is making it work for the individual teacher. Just as instruction needs to be unique to the needs of the students and each teacher's style of teaching, effective assessment needs to be tailored to the needs of each individual classroom. How will your comprehension assessment program look? Now is the time to explore comprehension assessment for your own teaching situation.

Plans for Change

Earlier in this chapter, you evaluated your own comprehension assessment strategies and, as a result, perhaps generated some ideas for change. Use the accompanying chart to make notes about the changes you wish to make. As you do so, make sure that these changes reflect the "big ideas" we outlined at the beginning of the section:

- Focus on critical information.
- Look for patterns of behavior.
- Recognize developmental progressions and attend to cultural differences.
- Be parsimonious. Which of your strategies will work for all of your students? Which might be reserved for more careful attention to some students' comprehension?
- Use instructional situations for assessment purposes.
- Include plans for (1) using assessment information to guide instruction and (2) sharing assessment information with children and parents.

You may want to share your plans with others to get their feedback.

Goal Planning: Comprehension Assessment

Goal _____

Plans by _____ Date _____

Action Steps: What do I need to do?	Materials/Resources	Evaluation: How will I assess the usefulness of this change?

70

Comprehension #1

You begin a discussion in science by asking a question. Three hands of three students go up: Jane, Bonita, and James. "Come on," you implore, "I'm sure some of the rest of you have ideas." Slowly, Mary and Jorge raise their hands. Jane, Bonita, James, Mary, and Jorge—the same five hands you always see.

At the beginning of the school year, you were pleased that the children participated in discussions. After a few weeks, though, you began to notice that the same five students seemed to be doing all the talking. So you decided to watch carefully, and you discovered that the "faithful five" discussed freely, but others seemed comfortable sitting back and listening (or pretending to listen).

You tried calling on other students. Although they generally responded appropriately, most answers were brief—the shortest answers they thought you'd tolerate. Besides that, calling on students seemed more like an oral quiz than true discussion or conversation.

Questions

- What kinds of questions do teachers ordinarily ask? What kinds of answers do they expect? What kinds of answers do students think teachers want?

- When do most people become eager to express their thoughts and ideas? When do they keep silent even though they have something to say?

- What can teachers do to encourage discussion?

Comprehension #2

You are a member of your district's Language Arts Committee, which undertakes a study of children's standardized test scores in reading. The group concludes that the "fourth-grade slump" may be a problem for children in the district. Many have sharply lower standardized test scores as they move from primary to intermediate grades.

The Language Arts Committee recommends that this finding be discussed at faculty meetings. When you invite discussion with your colleagues, it becomes apparent that primary teachers want to blame intermediate teachers for "the slump." Primary teachers express concerns about the extent to which intermediate-level instruction is appropriate for children. They believe that this inappropriate instruction leads to children's test difficulties.

The intermediate teachers, on the other hand, want to blame primary teachers. Specifically, they express concerns that primary-level instruction is so focused on decoding that comprehension receives little emphasis and, consequently, children perform poorly on intermediate-level tests of comprehension.

When you return to the Language Arts Committee to share your colleagues' perceptions about the issue, you find that other faculty discussions were similar. The Language Arts Committee must develop a plan to solve the problem of the "fourth-grade slump."

Questions

- Which group of teachers, primary or intermediate, has the better explanation for the test results? Why?
- Which group of teachers is responsible for attempting to solve this problem? Why?
- What role should comprehension instruction play in primary classrooms?
- How can teachers determine if their instruction is meeting children's needs?

CHAPTER 4

Beyond Strategies and Beyond the Classroom

*R*eading comprehension is the ultimate goal of reading and instruction in reading. Clearly, it needs to be a focal point of regular and systematic classroom instruction. However, comprehension is critical to overall school success, so teachers must work to make their instruction go beyond the classroom walls and into all parts of the school and beyond the school into the home. In this chapter we explore with you the opportunities and possibilities of moving comprehension instruction beyond the classroom.

We also consider issues that go beyond the implementation of instructional strategies in and beyond the classrooms. What kinds of texts should be used for comprehension instruction? How should students be grouped for instruction? And how do teachers work with children who find reading difficult and with those for whom English is not their first language (ELL students)?

Beyond the Classroom

We begin with the well-accepted notion that read-alouds need to be an integral of reading development at all ages and grades. Students need to see and hear good literature read to them. Although the commonsense idea of reading aloud to students is very appealing, the research behind reading aloud to students is also quite compelling (Rasinski, 2003). Research has demonstrated that one of the key characteristics of families in which children learn to read before starting school is parents who read to their children on a daily basis (Durkin, 1966). These parents read to their children voraciously in a way that the children can see the text while the parents read it to them. Similarly, research demonstrates that children in school who are read to regularly have larger vocabularies and are better comprehenders than students who are not read to in school on a regular basis (Cohen, 1968; Rasinski, 2003). Such a finding just makes good sense—students who are read to are often exposed to books and other material that are above their own reading level (indeed, scholars recommend that children be read material that is above their own reading level). Through exposure to higher-level material, children are presented with more sophisticated vocabulary and more complex plots and characters than they might read on their own. This type of exposure is sure to challenge students and lead to their working to make sense of what they read. Reading aloud to children builds vocabulary and comprehension, increases children's background knowledge on the topics of the material they hear read to them, models fluency in reading, and increases children's interest in books and reading and in the topics that they are exposed to through read-aloud material.

Thus, it should be a given that classroom teachers of all grade levels and content areas read to their students on a regular basis. Moreover, an equally compelling argument can (and should) be raised that teachers in the special areas such as physical education, library, art, and music should also read to students regularly. With the wealth and variety of books and other authentic texts for students—from sports, to music, to art, and more—excellent texts are available to meet any teacher's needs, topics, and interests. Moreover, that same recommendation to read to students should also apply directly to parents. If other teachers and parents read to children regularly, those students will be exposed to huge amounts of material that will challenge them to make meaning of what they read.

The reading comprehension strategies that we presented in Chapter 2 are intended for students to employ when they read on their own. However, it should be quite clear that students can use these very same strategies when they are read to by others. As children are read to, they can be prompted to engage in building images, developing predictions, and making connections to their own lives, the world in general, and to other reading material they have been exposed to earlier. Thus, it is crucial for us to communicate to teachers and parents the importance of reading aloud to children; it is also important that we help nurture in our teacher colleagues, parents, and others who may read to children the comprehension strategies that may help students learn to construct meaning as they read.

It may not be possible or appropriate to make parents and teachers who are not primarily reading teachers conversant with the full range of comprehension strategies. However, it certainly is reasonable to expect teachers and parents to become familiar with strategies that are of high value, particularly appropriate for various teachers and parents, and not overly complex to implement.

We suggest you work with other reading teachers, specialists, and coaches in your building to identify high-value strategies and to develop methods and materials to present to your colleagues and parents. Consider the following questions and points:

- What two or three reading comprehension strategies do you think would be most valuable for the school media specialist, the music teacher, the art teacher, the physical education teacher, the school principal, and parents to know? Are they the same strategies for each of these groups?

Book Club

- What reading materials are most appropriate for these various groups? You may wish to consult with or survey your colleagues and parents to find out the kinds of topics they find interesting and would like to share with their students and children. Are certain genres or text types more appropriate for some than others? Does informational text take priority over narrative? Can poetry work with a certain teacher? Are the materials most likely used from books, magazines, newspapers, or the Internet? Does a particular teacher tend to work more with graphs, charts, tables, maps, and other graphic information than with written texts? The kinds of materials a teacher or parent prefers will often dictate the comprehension strategy that he or she would find most useful. Try to identify the two or three comprehension strategies that a teacher or parent would find most useful.

- Are you able to make a list of specific reading and read-aloud material that a teacher or parent would find most appealing?

- After laying the groundwork by developing the information just mentioned, plan a professional development activity for teachers and parents in which they learn about the comprehension strategies that have the greatest value.

   1. What materials will you need to develop?

   2. Make a list of books and other recommended reading materials the teachers and parents can use with their students and children.

   3. The training should be no more than an hour. What will the agenda look like? We recommend the gradual release of responsibility model in which you, the instructor, present an overview of the strategy, model it with a student or colleague, give teachers and parents an opportunity to try it out with a student or colleague under your watchful and supportive eye, answer questions, and then have teachers and parents plan how they will actually implement what they have learned in their own classrooms or homes tomorrow.

Beyond Strategies

The strategies outlined in this book are critical to develop students' comprehension skills. They are approaches for helping students unlock content or acquire knowledge from written material. As significant as these are, it is also important to keep in mind other factors that need to be considered in comprehension instruction. Four factors that definitely need to be considered are the ones that are presented in the other books in this series; phonemic awareness, phonics and word decoding, reading fluency, and vocabulary are gateways to comprehension. Students need to have the skills and strategies associated with these factors in order to comprehend. In many cases, lack of comprehension comes from lack of proficiency in these other areas. Duke, Pressley, and Hilden (2004), for example, argue that for a substantial number of students who struggle in reading and reading comprehension, the source of the problem is not comprehension processing as much as it is difficulty with another factor associated with reading, such as word recognition and fluency. Thus, we view these other factors, the ones presented in the other books in this series, as ultimately reading comprehension factors that need to be taught in order to ensure reading comprehension.

Texts

The texts students are asked to read need to be considered for reading comprehension instruction. Material that is too challenging or unfamiliar for students will impede comprehension. Look for texts that are at the appropriate level of difficulty for students.

Texts can be measured for difficulty in a variety of ways called *readability formulas*. These methods for assessing difficulty examine the text for word and sentence difficulty and provide a numerical rating, often a grade-level score, that represents the appropriate level of difficulty for a particular book or passage. Several resources are available that allow teachers to determine readability. One favorite website is www.interventioncentral.org. At *Reading Probe Generator*, found on this website, you can enter a text segment, which the website will then analyze for its readability level using a well-established formula.

Another web resources is www.lexile.com. The authors of this website have calculated the lexile score, a highly regarded readability measure, for literally thousands of books for students. You simply type in the title and the website will provide you with a lexile score and a brief synopsis of the book.

Another simple way of determining whether a book or text may be appropriate for individual students is to have them read small portions of the text aloud. While they read, you mark any errors they make in their reading. Readers should make no more than five to seven uncorrected errors per 100 words on appropriately leveled text. Passages on which 8 percent or more of the words are read incorrectly and are uncorrected may be considered too difficult and may lead to poor comprehension.

Beyond the level of the texts, however, it is important to be aware of other text factors. One of the most important is type and genre of material students are asked to read. A wide variety of texts are available students, each having its own comprehension challenge. Ideally, students should become masters of as many text types as possible, and in order for that to happen they need to be exposed to as many types as possible. Certainly, stories or narrative texts are important. And there are many forms of narratives—contemporary fiction, historical fiction, fantasy, fairy tales, mysteries, and biographies to name a few.

Similarly, expository texts—texts meant to teach or provide content—are clearly important for students. These texts are organized in significantly different ways from stories and require different approaches for comprehension. Moreover, like narrative, exposition is made up of a variety of organizational forms, such as enumeration (listing information), chronological, compare-contrast, cause-effect, and problem-solution. To complicate things even more, most informational texts have embedded in them some or all of these forms.

In addition to narrative and exposition, which make up the bulk of school reading, there are many other text forms that students should be given opportunities to read and understand. Here is a listing of just a few (What other forms can you think of?):

- Poetry
- Letters
- Journals

- Scripts
- Oratory
- Maps, graphs, charts, tables

Each of these forms presents its own comprehension challenge to students; students will not have a chance to deal with these challenges unless they are exposed to these text forms.

Grouping

Instruction in school settings is rarely on an individual basis. Most instruction happens in groups, and the type of group that students find themselves in can affect learning outcomes. Should instruction be individual, small group, large group, homogeneous groups, heterogeneous groups, cross-age groups, or some other form of grouping? For reading comprehension purposes, our answer to this question is *yes*! We are strong advocates of flexible grouping. Life occurs in a variety of grouping situations; learning and reading comprehension does as well. Students should have the opportunity to learn in a number of grouping schemes. As a teacher, you need to think about how you can have multiple grouping schemes going on throughout the school day and how your grouping schemes can change from one day to the next, quickly and seamlessly. Some questions that may help you in determining how to group students for reading and reading comprehension instruction may include:

In what reading situations would I want students

- grouped according to similar reading levels?
- grouped according to similar interests?
- grouped according to similar needs?
- grouped in a variety of reading levels?
- in one large group?
- in similar-level, differential-level, or cross-age-level pairs or trios?
- working with me individually?
- working with an adult tutor, volunteer, or aide?

The answers to these questions should come from the purposes you have for reading; the nature of the reading itself (oral, silent, buddy reading, performance, assessment, read-aloud by the teacher or other adult); the type of text you are reading; and what you want students to do in response to the reading (discussion, writing, projects, performance, etc.). Other questions that need to be entertained include How large should the group be? and For what period of time should a group be kept together before it is changed?

Students need to see themselves working with their classmates in a variety of ways so that they can benefit from the opportunity to teach, learn from, get along with, and talk with their classmates as well as their teacher. The worst possible scenario in any classroom is to have one grouping system that never changes. It may be easy for the teacher, but it is deadly for students' minds.

Students with a Difference—Struggling Readers and English Language Learners

No matter what classroom you may find yourself in, you are going to have students who are different. Some are going to be more advanced than what is expected of their grade placement, some will be less advanced, and some will be profoundly less advanced. Some students will be different because of their cultural and linguistic background, and a disproportionate number of these students will be ones who will find learning to read difficult (Duke, Pressley, & Hilden, 2004). In particular, it is quite possible that many of your students will not speak English as their first language. Some of these students may be remarkably advanced in their learning of English, and others may be in the initial stages of acquiring English.

Regardless of who your students are, reading comprehension is essential to school success and independent learning, and the comprehension strategies outlined in Chapter 2 are the tools for making sense of text. No matter the type, nature, or level of students with whom you are working, *all* of them will benefit from a knowledge of strategies for comprehending text.

Although the nature and content of the comprehension strategies that are taught to students with a difference are the same as the ones taught with all students, there are other considerations that teachers need to be aware of in their work with these students. We present some of the major ones identified by research on effective intervention programs (Hiebert & Taylor, 1994; Pikulski, 1994; Snow, Burns, & Griffin, 1998). If they seem familiar to you, it is because we have discussed them in previous chapters and in other books in this series.

- *Gradual release of responsibility.* This concept is particularly relevant for students who, for whatever reason, struggle in learning to read. These students need additional support for more extended periods of time. The release of responsibility for employing a strategy must to be more gradual for this group of readers. The additional support can be provided in many ways—the following bullets identify a few.

- *Text choice.* Earlier in this chapter we identified text choice as an important consideration. This is particularly true for your students with a difference. These students may not be very good decoders and may not have wide backgrounds for the material you ask them to read. Thus, you need to be especially careful in selecting the materials you ask students to read, making doubly sure that the material is at the appropriate level of reading difficulty and that it is within the range of the students' interests and background knowledge.

  It may be that the material is too difficult for students and/or the students do not have sufficient background knowledge for the material. This is often the case, as you do not always have control over the materials students are expected to read. In these instances, you need to consider ways to make the actual reading of the text easier for students and ways to provide background knowledge so that students have something they can relate to the new material in the text. This could mean reading the text or a portion of the text to students, asking the students follow along silently while it is read to them, or having students listen to (and read along with) a prerecorded version of the text. Walters and Gunderson (1985) and Blum (1995) report reading achievement benefits for ELL students listening to texts read aloud to them in their first language and English.

Texts should be chosen that are carefully sequenced in difficulty so that students can gradually and successfully move their way through more challenging material. Difficulty, however, needs to be considered not only in terms of traditional readability (word and sentence difficulty) but also for content. Thematic text instruction in which one text provides background knowledge for the next text can allow for the sequential scaffolding that allows readers to achieve success. If the text choice is clearly challenging for students, it is up to the teacher to provide adequate support and scaffolding so that students can be successful. This may mean providing background and conceptual knowledge in advance of the reading.

- *Sequenced instruction.* Like texts, instruction is carefully sequenced so that students work with simple examples of a concept with plenty of teacher support. The students will gradually move to progressively more complex work with the instructional concept, and the teacher will provide progressively less support.

- *Patterned and businesslike lesson structures.* Lessons should be structured so that they follow a regular routine or pattern from day to day. This allows students to understand the general structure of the lesson so that every activity within the lesson does not have to be introduced and explained daily. Time is used for focused instruction on the comprehension strategy, not explanation of how to do the instructional activity. Moreover, the lessons are businesslike in nature—fast paced and to the point. Minimal time is used for small talk and sidebar conversations. Instruction is focused solely on the task at hand and the concepts to be taught.

- *Instruction in the context of authentic reading.* The strategies and skills to be learned are taught through real reading of authentic reading material—real literature. After the strategies and skills are taught, they are immediately applied in purposeful reading of authentic literature.

- *Small group and individualized instruction.* Students who are having difficulty with reading and understanding what they read need more focused attention. This can be facilitated when the teacher is able to work with smaller groups (five to seven students) or individuals.

The strategies students use to comprehend what they read are the content that needs to be the focus of your instruction. How, when, and under what conditions that instruction takes place is another set of considerations. As you plan for your own strategy instruction with students, we hope that you will think about these other factors that can mean the difference between success and disappointment in helping students learn to make meaning out of what they read.

ACED: Analysis, Clarification, Extension, Discussion

I. REFLECTION (10 to 15 minutes)

ANALYSIS:

- What, for you, were the most interesting and/or important ideas in this chapter?

  _____

  _____

  _____

  _____

- What information was new to you (or different from your own prior knowledge)?

  _____

  _____

  _____

  _____

CLARIFICATION:

- Did anything surprise you? Confuse you? Cause you to stop and reflect?

  _____

  _____

  _____

  _____

- Was there anything missing from or overlooked in this presentation?

  _____

  _____

  _____

  _____

EXTENSION:

- What new questions or wonderings do you have?

  _____

  _____

  _____

  _____

- Can you relate any information presented in this chapter to your own previous teaching experiences or to students you have taught in the past?

  _____

  _____

  _____

  _____

- What new insights did you develop as a result of reading this chapter?

  _____

  _____

  _____

  _____

II. DISCUSSION (20 minutes)

- Form groups of 4 to 6 members.

- Appoint a *facilitator (timer)* and *recorder.*

- Share responses. Make sure that each person has shared his or her responses to each category (Analysis/Clarification/Extension).

- Help each other with any areas of confusion.

- Answer and/or discuss questions raised by group members.

- On chart paper, the recorder should summarize the main discussion points and identify issues or questions the group would like to raise for general discussion.

III. APPLICATION (10 minutes)

- Based on your reflection and discussion, how might you apply what you have learned from this chapter?

_____

_____

_____

_____

CHAPTER 5

Resources

World Wide Web Resources for Comprehension

www.literacy.uconn.edu/compre.htm. At this website, developed at the University of Connecticut, reading comprehension processes are divided into three categories: vocabulary instruction, text comprehension instruction, and comprehension strategies. You'll also find useful websites that students can visit to practice their use of comprehension strategies with fiction and nonfiction texts at a variety of reading levels.

www.resourceroom.net/Comprehension/index.asp. This website contains a collection of lessons and articles that deal with various aspects of reading comprehension.

www.readinga-z.com/newfiles/preview.html. This commercially sponsored website is a repository of online books that are supported by guided reading lessons.

www.readingquest.org/strat/. At this website you will find lessons, strategies, and materials designed to foster reading comprehension, particularly in the social studies.

www.muskingum.edu/~cal/database/general/reading.html. This website provides teachers with a set of general and specific strategies and ideas for teaching comprehension, particularly with those students who experience difficulty in learning from text.

Professional Resources for Teachers

Beck, I. L., & McKeown, M. G. (2006). *Improving comprehension with questioning the author.* New York: Scholastic.

Block, C. C., Gambrell, L., & Pressley, M. (Eds.). (2002). *Improving reading comprehension: Rethinking research, theory, and classroom practice.* San Francisco: Jossey Bass.

Block, C. C., & Pressley, M. (Eds.). (2001). *Comprehension instruction: Research-based best practices.* New York: Guilford.

Cooper, J. D. (1986). *Improving reading comprehension.* Boston: Houghton Mifflin.

Cooper, J. D. (2006). *Literacy: Helping children construct meaning* (6th ed.). Boston: Houghton Mifflin.

Daniels, H. (1994). *Literature circles: Voice and choice in the student-centered classroom.* Portland, ME: Stenhouse.

Day, J. P., Spiegel, D. L., McLellan, J., & Brown, V. B. (2002). *Moving forward with literature circles.* New York: Scholastic.

Harvey, S. (1998). *Nonfiction matters: Reading, writing, and research in grades 3-8.* Portland, ME: Stenhouse.

Harvey, S., & Goudvis, A. (2000). *Strategies that work.* Portland, ME: Stenhouse.

Hoyt, L. (1998). *Revisit, reflect, retell: Strategies for improving reading comprehension.* Portsmouth, NH: Heinemann.

McLaughlin, M. (2003). *Guided comprehension in the primary grades.* Newark, DE: International Reading Association.

McLaughlin, M., & Allen, M. B. (2002). *Guided comprehension in action: A teaching model for grades 3-8.* Newark, DE: International Reading Association.

McLaughlin, M., & Allen, M. B. (2002). *Guided comprehension in action: Lessons for grades 3-8.* Newark, DE: International Reading Association.

McLaughlin, M., & DeVoogd, G. (2004) *Critical literacy: Enhancing students' comprehension of text.* New York: Scholastic.

Miller, D. (2002). *Reading with meaning: Teaching comprehension in the primary grades.* Portland, ME: Stenhouse.

Rasinski, T. V., Padak, N. D., et al. (2000). *Teaching comprehension and exploring multiple literacies: Strategies from The Reading Teacher.* Newark, DE: International Reading Association.

Wilhelm, J. D. (1996). *You gotta BE the book: Teaching engaged and reflective reading with adolescents.* New York: Teachers College Press.

Wilhelm, J. D. (2001). *Improving comprehension with think-aloud strategies.* New York: Scholastic.

Wilhelm, J. D. (2002) *Action strategies for deepening comprehension: Role plays, text structure, tableaux, talking statues, and other enrichment techniques that engage students with text.* New York: Scholastic.

Wilhelm, J., Baker, T., & Dube, J. (2001). *Strategic reading: Guiding students to lifelong literacy.* Portsmouth, NH: Heinemann.

Book Club Ideas

Book Club

Throughout the book, you have seen icons indicating activities or discussion points that lend themselves to book club conversations. We hope you and your colleagues will take advantage of these opportunities. Our experience has taught us that learning from and with each other is a powerful way to promote innovation. In this appendix, we provide additional questions and ideas for discussion. They are organized according to the chapters in the book.

Introduction: Reading Comprehension

- Look more closely at the reading comprehension chapter in the report of the National Reading Panel. Make notes about key insights and the classroom implications of these insights. Share these with colleagues. (The report is available online at www.nationalreadingpanel.org. For a shorter version go to www.nifl.gov/partnershipforreading/publications/PEDbookletBW.pdf.)
- Select a piece of follow-up reading from the NRP website or at the National Institute for Literacy (http://nifl.gov). Make notes and share these with your colleagues.
- Think back to the beginning of your teaching career. What were you taught about teaching reading comprehension? Share these insights with colleagues and together attempt to determine how the role of reading comprehension in early literacy instruction has changed over time.

Book Club

Chapter 1: Reading Comprehension: Definitions, Research, and Considerations

- Reading comprehension is not simply the recall of information encountered in text. It is the construction of the meaning of the text that the reader builds based on his or her prior knowledge. After reading this chapter make notes about key insights and the classroom implications of these insights. Share these with colleagues.

- Make notes about the relationship between reading comprehension and the background or prior knowledge that readers bring to the reading task. With your colleagues, write a paragraph that explains this relationship.

- Select one of the studies referenced in the chapter. Read it, make notes about it, and share these with your colleagues.

- Think about any passage(s) that you have ever read for which you either had little background knowledge or were not aware that you should be using it. Make notes about this experience, and share your thoughts with your colleagues.

- With your colleagues, think about how can you actively involve your students in making decisions, solving problems, and using background knowledge in an attempt for them to make sense of the passages they read in your classroom.

- Think about some strategies you may use in your classroom to help students make sense of and connect what they read with prior information they have. Share your ideas with your colleagues.

- Brainstorm with colleagues ways to increase your emphasis on reading comprehension instruction throughout the school day. Make concrete plans for integrating these ideas into your instructional routines.

Chapter 2: Instructional Strategies for Reading Comprehension

- Decide on the two or three instructional activities best suited for your classroom. Explain to your colleagues why each activity is a good fit.
- For each activity selected, make plans for implementation. Keep track of questions. Share your plans with colleagues and discuss questions.
- For each activity selected, make plans to assess impact. That is, how will you determine if these new activities are enhancing your students' reading comprehension? Share your ideas with colleagues and invite them to offer feedback.
- Talk with colleagues about how you can draw attention to reading comprehension during teacher read-alouds and students' guided reading lessons.
- If you are currently using a commercial reading comprehension program, evaluate it using the questions posed at the end of the chapter. If your evaluation identifies weaknesses, discuss these with your colleagues. Make plans to strengthen these weak areas, if possible.

Chapter 3: Assessing Reading Comprehension

- Discuss each "big idea" about assessment in more detail. Decide if you agree or disagree with each, why, and what implications the ideas have for your classroom assessment plans for reading comprehension.
- List all possible revisions to your classroom assessment plans for reading comprehension. Then rank-order these. Explain your reasoning to your colleagues.
- For the most important revision idea from the activity above, develop an implementation plan. Share this with your colleagues and seek their feedback.

Chapter 4: Beyond Strategies and Beyond the Classroom

- Develop detailed notes about the following: How do you currently explain reading comprehension to parents? What do you currently do to help parents see the role they play in promoting their children's reading comprehension?
- Review the chapter's suggested activities for supporting a child's reading comprehension at home. Select those activities that you believe would be useful and feasible for the families of your students. Make detailed plans for sharing the activities you selected with these families. For example, draft a newsletter that includes suggested reading comprehension activities or plan a parent workshop that models home-based reading comprehension activities.
- Outline your current parent-teacher conference format. Discuss the strengths and weaknesses of this format. Based on the suggestions offered in the chapter, and on your conversations with colleagues, consider revisions you could make to your conferences in order to increase their effectiveness.

Chapter 5: Resources

- Review the lists of websites provided in Chapter 5 for helping students practice their use of comprehension strategies with fiction and nonfiction texts. Select two or more of these useful websites to share with your students. Make plans for incorporating these sources in your instructional plans.
- The chapter provides lists of websites for supporting reading comprehension. Discuss with colleagues other useful sources that you could add to these lists. Discuss suggestions for ways in which these sources can be used with students
- Search the Reading Quest website for additional lessons, strategies, and materials that can provide support for reading comprehension instruction.
- With your colleagues, select a different professional book from the list in Chapter 5. Read and summarize the book (or a portion of the book) for your colleagues. Listen to reports on other books by your colleagues. Try to distill important insights from the various resources that were shared.

Notes

*A*s you work through the book, you may want to make notes here about important ideas gleaned from discussions. You can keep track of additional resources. You may also want to use these pages to reflect on changes you made in your comprehension instruction and to make notes about next steps.

General Issues and Ideas

Instructional Plans

Assessment Plans

Working with Home Partners

Resources for Teachers

APPENDIX B

Notes

References

Adams, M., & Bertram, B. (1980). *Background knowledge and reading comprehension*. Reading Education Report No. 13. Urbana, IL: University of Illinois Center for the Study of Reading. (ERIC Document Reproduction Service No. ED 181 431).

Anderson, R. C., & Pearson, P. D. (1984). A schema-theoretic view of basic processes in reading comprehension. In P. D. Pearson (Ed.), *Handbook of reading research* (pp. 255–291). New York: Longman.

Beck, I., McKeown, M., & Kucan, L. (2002). *Bringing words to life: Robust vocabulary instruction*. New York: Guilford.

Blum, I. (1995). Using audiotaped books to extend classroom literacy instruction into the homes of second-language learners. *Journal of Reading Behavior, 27*, 535–563.

Brown, M. W. (1990). *The important book*. New York: Harper Trophy.

Clymer, T. (1968). What is "reading"? Some current concepts. In H. M. Robinson (Ed.), *Innovation and chance in reading instruction. Sixty-seventh Yearbook of the National Society of the Study of Education*. Chicago: University of Chicago Press.

Cohen, D. (1968). The effect of literature on vocabulary and comprehension. *Elementary English, 45*, 209–213, 217.

Daniels, H. (2002). *Literature circles: Voice and choice in book clubs and reading groups* (2nd ed.). Portland, ME: Stenhouse.

Darling-Hammond, L., & McLaughlin, M. W. (1995). Policies that support professional development in an era of reform. *Phi Delta Kappan, 76*, 597–604.

Duke, N. K., Pressley, M., & Hilden, K. (2004). Difficulties in reading comprehension. In C. A. Stone, E. R. Silliman, B. J. Ehren, & K. Apel (Eds.), *Handbook of language and literacy: Development and disorders* (pp. 501–520). New York: Guilford.

Durkin, D. (1966). *Children who read early*. New York: Teachers College Press.

Durkin, D. (1978). What is the value of the new interest in reading comprehension? *Language Arts, 58*, 23–43.

Durkin, D. (1981). Reading comprehension in five basal reader series. *Reading Research Quarterly, 16,* 515–544.

Gardner, H. (2000). *Intelligence reframed: Multiple intelligences for the 21st century.* New York: Basic Books.

Hall, D. (1994). *I am the dog, I am the cat.* New York: Dial.

Harris, T. L., & Hodges, R E. (Eds.). (1995). *The literacy dictionary: The vocabulary of reading and writing.* Newark, DE: International Reading Association.

Harvey, S., & Goudvis, A. (2000). *Strategies that work.* Portland, ME: Stenhouse.

Hesse, K. (1997). *Out of the dust.* New York: Scholastic.

Hiebert, E., & Taylor, B. M. (1994). *Getting reading right from the start: Effective early literacy interventions.* Boston: Allyn & Bacon.

Hoffman, J. V. (1992). Critical reading/thinking across the curriculum: Using I Charts to support learning. *Language Arts, 69,* 121–127.

Marzano, R., Pickering, D., & Pollock, J. (2001). *Classroom instruction that works: Research-based strategies for increasing student achievement.* Alexandria, VA: Association for Supervision and Curriculum Development.

McMahon, S., & Raphael, T. (1997). *The book club connection: Literacy learning and classroom talk.* New York: Teachers College Press.

McTighe, J., & Wiggins, G. (2004). *Understanding by design.* Alexandria, VA: Association for Supervision and Curriculum Development.

Moore, D. W., & Moore, S. A. (1986). Possible sentences. In E. K. Dishner, T. W. Bean, J. E. Readence, & D. W. Moore (Eds.), *Reading in the content areas: Improving classroom instruction* (2nd ed.) (pp. 174–179). Dubuque, IA: Kendall/Hunt.

National Reading Panel. (2000). *Report of the National Reading Panel: Teaching children to read. Report of the subgroups.* Washington, DC: U.S. Department of Health and Human Services, National Institutes of Health.

Noe, K., & Johnson, N. (1999). *Getting started with literature circles.* Norwood, MA: Christopher Gordon.

Pearson, P. D., et al. (1979). *The effect of background knowledge on young children's comprehension of explicit and implicit information.* Urbana, IL: University of Illinois, Center for the Study of Reading.

Pearson, P. D., & Gallagher, M. C. (1983). The instruction of reading comprehension. *Contemporary Educational Psychology, 8,* 317–344.

Pikulski, J. J. (1994). Preventing reading failure: A review of five effective programs. *The Reading Teacher, 48,* 30–39.

Pressley, M., & McDonald-Wharton, R. (2002). The need for increased comprehension instruction. In M. Pressley (Ed.), *Reading instruction that works* (2nd ed.) (pp. 236–288). New York: Guilford.

Rasinski, T. V. (2003). *The fluent reader: Oral reading strategies for building word recognition, fluency, and comprehension.* New York: Scholastic.

Rasinski, T. V., & Padak, N. (2004). *Effective reading strategies: Teaching children who find reading difficult* (3rd ed.). Upper Saddle River, NJ: Pearson.

Renyi, J. (1998). Building learning into the teaching job. *Educational Leadership, 55*(5), 70–74.

Rumelhart, D. E. (1980). Schemata: The building blocks of cognition. In R. J. Spiro, B. C. Bruce, & W. F. Brewer (Eds.), *Theoretical issues in reading comprehension* (pp. 33–58). Hillsdale, NJ: Erlbaum.

Snow, C., Burns, M. S., & Griffin, P. (Eds.). (1998). *Preventing reading difficulties in young children.* Washington, DC: National Academy Press.

Stahl S. A., & Kapinus, B. A. (1991). Possible sentences: Predicting word meanings to teach content vocabulary. *The Reading Teacher, 40,* 62–69.

Stauffer, R. (1980). *The language-experience approach to the teaching of reading* (2nd ed.). New York: Harper & Row.

Tierney, R. (1998). Literacy assessment reform: Shifting beliefs, principled possibilities, and emerging practices. *The Reading Teacher, 51,* 374–390.

Walters, K., & Gunderson, L. (1985). Effects of parent volunteers reading first language (L1) books to ESL students. *The Reading Teacher, 39,* 66–69.

Wenglinsky, H. (2000). *How teaching matters: Bringing the classroom back into discussions of teacher quality.* Princeton, NJ: Educational Testing Service.

West, K. (1998). Noticing and responding to learners: Literacy evaluation and instruction in the primary grades. *The Reading Teacher, 51,* 550–559.